A MEMOIR

Gratitude

LAURA STEENROD

authorHOUSE®

AuthorHouse™
1663 Liberty Drive
Bloomington, IN 47403
www.authorhouse.com
Phone: 1 (800) 839-8640

Published by AuthorHouse   03/30/2017

ISBN: 978-1-5246-8522-5 (sc)
ISBN: 978-1-5246-8521-8 (e)

Library of Congress Control Number: 2017904477

Print information available on the last page.

Any people depicted in stock imagery provided by Thinkstock are models,
and such images are being used for illustrative purposes only.
Certain stock imagery © Thinkstock.

This book is printed on acid-free paper.

Because of the dynamic nature of the Internet, any web addresses or
links contained in this book may have changed since publication and
may no longer be valid. The views expressed in this work are solely those
of the author and do not necessarily reflect the views of the publisher,
and the publisher hereby disclaims any responsibility for them.

For My Mother

Acknowledgements

My deepest appreciation to author, mentor and friend, Wade Rouse and his spouse, Gary Edwards, for sharing your knowledge, support, and, on several occasions, your home while this book manifested. I could not have done this without you. To Linda Bayliss, for your tireless editing, hand-holding and patience, teaching me everything I never paid attention to in high school English class. To Nan, for listening to me read aloud as we drove across the country laughing and crying. To Nakita Hammond-Tuthill, for capturing the magic and beauty of the animals with your camera and unselfishly sharing it. To all of my family and friends, for your unconditional love and support, especially Abigail and Carter, for the many times when you were my reason for putting one foot in front of the other. To my husband, Denny, for putting up with three decades of my special kind of crazy, sharing our lives covered in and surrounded by dog hair and for always loving me, even when I test the limits. And lastly, to all the animals, for the overwhelming abundance and light you bring into my life.

Love

The trouble is, you think you have time.
~ Buddha

Winter 2010

"You can't change an exit," I say to my mom from the passenger seat of her car. We are just a few minutes into our weekly outing which consists of three of our mutually favorite things: food, spending money and caffeine. On this particular Friday morning, my mother is somewhat baffled and deeply saddened as she shares the news of the unexpected death of a woman who had been both her and my grandmother's friend.

"You really don't think we have any control over death?" my mother asks. It is both a comment and a question.

"It's not that we don't have control over death, Mom. Certainly people have demonstrated that there's control over physical death since the beginning of time. I think we come into this lifetime with planned exits. When the time is right... and I don't mean human timing, I mean a time supported by the Universe...we leave." I take a deep breath and continue. "I have never heard anyone question the perfection of the moment any of us arrived into this lifetime; I honestly don't believe the moment we leave is any less perfect." My mother sighs and reaches over to gently pat my hand.

As mom and I head into town, the first stop is our favorite little "hole-in-the-wall" diner where we will split an omelet the size of my thigh. "Oh, my goodness. This is huge!" My mother says every time we eat here, and then we will both proceed to clean up our plates. As is customary, we will chase the giant morning meal with a sugar-laden latte from the Starbucks drive-thru and then begin to tackle our list of assorted errands. Our "To Do's" vary from week to week but always involve some sort of shopping; it's what we do best. On more than one occasion we have found ourselves involved in an adventure of some kind, like the time my mother drove behind me, four-ways flashing while I chased a lost and frightened German Shepherd puppy down a four lane road.

My mother usually has a morning monologue airing the frustrations related to being married to my father. Our conversations are always easy and comfortable. We have, somewhere along the way, grown into the habit of sharing our emotional lives with each other. This relationship is a safe place for us both, although I will occasionally say to her, "Don't say anything to dad," or, "this isn't something to share with your sewing girlfriends." She will smile and say, "I wasn't going to, sweetie," and I always smile back, "*yes*, you were."

"I'm sorry you're sad today," I reach across and rub my mom's shoulder as we climb back into her car after breakfast, and she instantly tears up.

"Thank you, honey," my mom replies. "I just feel so bad for her family and her friends."

"I'm quite sure it absolutely sucks to be the one left behind. Do you want to run over to the mall?" The question is my transparent attempt to get her mind on something else.

"I think we should," my mom says and gives the steering wheel a quick smack with the palm of her hand. "Let's get going!" and we are off.

Shopping is an effortless activity for both of us. Wherever we go, from the Dollar Store to Macy's, we always find something to spend our money on. We are both addicted to--and experts at--acquiring items, and since I extinguished all my "big addictions" several years ago, I enjoy it. Unlike my mother, though, I am a compulsive returner. That way, I get to feel good about the item twice!

Our mother-daughter ritual was originally born out of my psychological crumbling in my late twenties. Over a span of about two years, I experienced a series of unsettling events: being held hostage and threatened at gunpoint during an armed robbery, a contentious divorce, whirlwind re-marriage and the death of my grandmother, who had been my anchor in the turbulent emotional sea of my early adulthood. Life had set mammoth speed bumps in front of me manifesting as anxiety and panic disorder. One thing became abundantly clear: my appreciation and understanding of the meaning of my life was ripe for a long and arduous growth spurt.

My worst moments of debilitation have been triggered while driving alone. These episodes cause my palms to sweat, my heart to grip painfully in my chest and taking a deep breath becomes a frantic struggle. I am unequipped to deal with the Tyrannosaurus Rex-sized fear that chases me. During those terrifying moments, my perception of the world looks and feels akin to the warped and distorted images that appear in the fun house mirrors at the county fair. I often feel like a character in a movie pursued by an unknown stalker, with tragedy or insanity lurking around the next corner. I could never clearly identify this dark and ominous predator, but its presence in my life would at times scare the living hell out of me.

I have been lucky. My family has been supportive even though incapacitating anxiety defies appropriate explanation for anyone who has never suffered from it. Ironically those of us whose personalities seem to make us the least likely candidates for such an affliction --- usually controlling, perfectionist, extroverted types--- are exactly those most susceptible to this sort of condition. Whenever I am sharing my story with people regarding my anxiety issues, I always tell them: The Universe saw the need to give me a "pop quiz" I've titled: What's Really in **Your** Control? One of my mother's greatest gifts to me during this turbulent and confusing time in my life has been her easy company. She never once acts disappointed, baffled or annoyed at the changes in me. She supports who I am on any given day. She is a gift.

I am an emotional infant. I am crippled, frightened and vulnerable but also acutely aware, almost from the onset, that I alone am responsible for how this struggle will define and shape me. I reflect back to my childhood and realize that these threads of fear and uncertainty have been trailing along behind me for a very long time, largely unnoticed until they have snagged and dragged along with them so much other debris, they can no longer be ignored. There are two things I am certain of while treading desperately to keep my head above this murky water: first, I alone am responsible for my own emotional and spiritual survival. Second, there is no salvation in being a victim.

Through the practice of meditation and observation, along with the never-ending reading and listening to spiritual literature, and the raw, tom-girl fight in me, the fearful feelings have dissipated over the years to a much less frightening, sometimes completely unnoticed, Labrador-sized fear that is often at the periphery of my awareness. Never driving a car alone, however, has become a lingering habit despite the fact that I identified my terrifying, mystery stalker years ago as my own psyche.

I pride myself on being somewhat intuitive, but on this ordinary Friday I do not have even the slightest inkling, after having resolutely shared my spiritual convictions on this bitter cold February morning and kissed my mom on the cheek before she pulled out of my driveway, that my faith in my theory of life and my spiritual growth would be put to the ultimate test, when five uneventful days later, my mother would literally drop dead.

February 23, 2010.
The Only Date I Remember,
Other Than My Birthday

Oddly enough, when my phone rings on that Wednesday afternoon, and I see my mom's name on the caller ID, I answer it. Normally, I would not. Both of my parents are well aware that on weekdays, especially after school hours, my horse farm will be bustling with public lesson students, private clients and a revolving door of horses in and out of the arena. Because these people are paying me for my undivided attention and instruction, unless my dad catches me in a brief reprieve between lessons, I will send the call to voicemail, and he always leaves a message. This lesson is in full swing, but for some reason, this time, I pick up.

There is one of three "me's" that will answer this particular call: Annoyed Me, with short, clipped tones; Patronizing Me, who sounds like I'm talking to a pre-schooler; or Bitchy Me with a "What's up, Dad?"

"Yeah, Dad" I say. Apparently, Patronizing Me is the one answering today. I envision that my mother is most likely scowling at him from somewhere close by, admonishing him for the hundredth time about calling me at this time of day, and he is glaring back defiantly doing so anyway.

Usually, the minute my dad hears me pick up, before I can spit out a word, he will already be saying, "I know you're teaching lessons….." But that is not what I hear. For a second or two, I don't hear anything.

"Dad?" I am slightly annoyed but also instantly alerted to this change in protocol.

"I need to tell you something. I need you to be brave." I hear my father choking back sobs. "Your mother……. is dead."

I am momentarily stunned. "What did you just say to me?" "What do mean my mom is dead?" I immediately feel a sense of panic wash over me, and everything around me fades into dark, muted tones. It is just me and my phone, which I am clutching with two hands as I walk in circles like a beheaded zombie.

"She's dead, Laura" he says again, and I am sinking to my knees on the sandy floor of my indoor riding arena.

"You need to get here," my father pleads. "I have to hang up and call your brother. You need to get here……" and the line goes dead.

One of my closest friends is squatting down beside me. Before my dad's call, she has been sitting on her horse along with several other riders. I do not see or hear anything other than her voice when she asks me, "Where is Denny?"

"At his parents," I answer dully.

I stare at my phone, trying to focus on what I need to do. It takes me a minute to remember my mother-and father in-law's last name. It is my last name, too. I call their home phone because Denny rarely answers his cell phone. My mother-in-law answers. "I need to talk to Denny," I sob into the phone.

"What's the matter, Laura?" my mother-in-law asks in a low voice.

"My mom is dead" I respond.

"How is your mom dead?" she asks in shocked disbelief.

"I don't know. My dad just called." I am moaning now and leaning into my friend, who is standing next to me, "I need to find Denny, I need to talk to Denny" I say again.

"Denny isn't here, Laura," says my mother-in-law, and I disconnect the call.

My girlfriend wraps her arms around me and pulls me up off the arena floor. She tells someone to put her horse away and walks me through the barn and up to the house. There is the usual commotion from the dogs when I walk into the house, but it dissipates quickly. My energy is obviously off, and they turn away from me almost immediately despite their love of company in the house. Denny is sitting at the kitchen table and stands up as soon as he sees me.

"My mom is dead," I tell my husband who is moving toward me.

"What?" he asks, sounding incredulous as I move toward him. He reaches to put his arms around me. I stop him and take a hold of his forearms, "We have to leave," I say dully, as I turn away from him and head for the door.

Sitting in the car, I call one of our closest family friends. She is a longtime surrogate sister and daughter to our family. She lives in the same complex as my parents. We don't talk on the phone often, and I can hear the delight in her voice that I am calling. I tell her I need her to listen carefully to what I am going to tell her. "On no, Laura, oh no, not mom," I am aware of the anguish in her voice. This is the second time in her life she is hearing the news of the unexpected death of a mother over the phone. I end our brief exchange with a directive to please get to my dad as quickly as possible. The rest of the family is being notified and will arrive as soon as we can.

"Not my mom, not my mom, not my mom," becomes my pleading mantra during the fifteen-minute ride to my parents' home. When we arrive, my father and friend meet us at the door, and we are all sobbing, except for the Sheriff's deputy and my parent's beagle, who are both solemnly standing by. "Where is she?" I manage to ask, hyperventilating.

"In her sewing room," my father answers. He is choking on his words and frantically wiping at the tears flowing from his eyes. "I tried to save her, Laura," my father says in an agonizing tone, "I couldn't save her….. I couldn't save her."

My mother is lying on the floor of her much-loved sewing room. It is actually a space on the ground floor of their condo that has been sectioned off by a floor-to-ceiling china cabinet acting as a partial wall. Her large sewing table is in the corner. The longest part of the table is where her prized sewing machine sets, with a view out the large windows that face the wooded lot at the rear of the condo. I believe my mother loves this space more than any other space she has ever had. She is always remarking about the deer that wander in and the large groups of wild turkey that parade obliviously past her window. This is a space where her heart speaks through the creation of magnificent quilts and Christmas tree skirts. This is also a place I believe she finds a comforting solitude, however brief, away from her children and our father.

If not for my mother's dead body on the floor, you would not know a tragedy had just occurred in this room.

Everything is exactly as it would be if she were sitting here creating or taking a break to make a cup of coffee. The phone sits in its cradle to the right of the sewing machine, not even a full arm's length from her chair. There is an open box of straight pins sitting undisturbed, a few inches in front of the phone, where she could easily pluck them out while she is working on her project. Nothing is out of place, except my mother. I am on my knees next to her body and lightly stroking her cheek with my fingers. The expression on my mother's face can only be described as placid. I am sobbing. "How did you find her, Dad?"

My father takes a ragged breath to steady himself. Normally, like so many men of his era, it is his habit to clear his throat and drop his voice an octave before answering a question, but that is not how he responds today. His voice is squeaky, strained and tinged with panic. "We went to lunch at Applebee's. She was fine. When we came home, she dropped me off because she had a haircut appointment. When she got home, she said she was going to go downstairs to work on her quilt," He takes another deep breath. "The phone rang, but she didn't answer it, so I did. I got up and hollered down the stairs to her.......she was only home maybe fifteen minutes or so......," he shakes his head and a choking sob escapes. He uses his sleeve to wipe the tears flowing down his face and his runny nose and then continues, "She didn't answer me, and so I said, "hang on a minute while I take the phone downstairs to my wife." When I walked in here……….. she was…………. leaning over on the table with her head down, and I shook her and said, "Pat." "I told the lady on the phone," his voice is high pitched, strained and cracking, and he is taking short, quick breaths, "I have to hang up because there is something wrong with my wife. I need to call 911', and I called 911," my dad looks directly at my husband as he says this, making a subconscious connection between my husband being a police officer and his desperate plea for assistance, "I said......I need help..........my wife...........she needs help." I can hear the pleading in his voice. "The girl asks me if I know CPR, and I said, 'Yes,' She tells me to put her on the floor and start CPR, and there is an ambulance on the way." Momentarily there is a pause in my dad's recounting. "I couldn't save her," he is sobbing and begins to hyperventilate, "I............ couldn't ....save.........her." My husband, tears streaming down his face as well, moves next to my father and puts his arm around his shoulder. I lower myself to sit down next to my mother's body and turn back to my dad.

"Mom wasn't here to be saved, Dad....... she was already gone," my own voice sounding foreign to my ears, "I can tell by the look on her face. Look how peaceful her face is, Dad" I turn toward her body and cup her cold cheek. I have already interpreted her almost-pleased expression as a validation. "She didn't push her chair away from the table to get up and get help. She never even disturbed the open box of pins sitting right next to her" I am aware that on my face is an anguished smile, and my own voice is coming out halting and reedy as my words catch in my throat. I do not bother to wipe away the tears that are rolling down my face and hanging suspended from my jawline. I have no idea if my dad is listening to me or if my words hold any measure of solace for him. My mother's death, I am absolutely certain, was immediate and without fear or struggle.

Life Goes On?

The first day following the worst day of my life, we all gather at what is now our father's home. How strange it is to reflexively pull out my cell phone and then remember that I cannot call my mom to tell her that she has died! She was always my go-to girl, especially whenever anything monumental happened, and this is monumental!

I spend more time in the company of my family than I ever have before. The absence of my mother makes our gathering feel like we are all riding together downhill in a wagon that's missing a wheel, precariously balanced and one bad move away from complete chaos. Just like in the movies, food begins arriving at the door. We are told who the senders are, but I at least, do not pay attention. Whatever coping mechanisms are coming into play for each one of us during this intensely stressful time, abstaining from food is not one of them. We are a food- loving family, and, as far as I know, everyone eats. I go through my mom's appointment calendar and make the necessary calls to cancel appointments. The receptionist at the chiropractor's office, who also knows me, says she hopes everything is O.K. and would my mom like to re-schedule? I tell her, "No, everything is not O.K. My mother died very unexpectedly yesterday." The receptionist gasps, "ohhhh noooo! I am so sorry......" she is noticeably shaken by the news. "**Please** send our condolences to Pat's family."

"Thank You," I say and hang up.

Two dogs call this condo home. Little Bear, a male Lhasa Apso, is glued to my father's lap while he sits in his recliner and stares blankly at the TV screen. The shaggy little dogs' protruding under-bite, crooked teeth and brief stint as the local pet shop display window make me suspect his origin is most likely a down-South puppy mill. The other dog is Sarah, an ancient, obese, tri-colored beagle. She has been stuck to me like a shadow since my arrival here this morning. My husband refers to her as the, "walking ottoman." I have been absently stroking her head while making phone calls and exchanging brief, dull conversation with family members as they wander in and out of the kitchen.

Sarah has lived with my parents for several years now, so it is not surprising that she knows something is seriously amiss. Her normal "*modus operandi*," especially when food is present, is to perpetually stroll, belly swaying back and forth, looking for a fallen morsel or a generous offering. As we sit together in the kitchen, me at table and her on the floor, leaning her ample weight against my right leg, she repeatedly glances up at me and asks, "Where is the mom? What is happening?" Of course, she is looking to me for answers, because this beagle and I have a history. She was once part of my dog pack.

Survival

Sometimes even to live is an act of courage.
~ Seneca

Sarah 2006

When new tenants move in to the rental property next to my farm, my heart sinks as I watch them pound a metal stake at the farthest reaches of the property line and attach a female beagle to it. I agonize watching her live long days on a short, weighty metal chain. The first day after their arrival, when my mother picks me up for a morning of errand running, I am fired up. "Do you see that, Mom? Do you see that goddamned dog staked over there?" I gesture wildly. "I can't even imagine what kind of piece of shit thinks that's O.K." I throw myself back in the seat of her Nissan, slapping my hands on my thighs.

"It's very sad," my mother says thoughtfully. "Is there anything we can do?"

"Probably not. This is a very rural, hands-off type of township," I sigh, "especially since she's a hunting breed."

The beagle's solitary location puts her closer to one of the large pole barn structures on my property than to the house where her people live. Her good days consist of blatant neglect; with endless hours of isolation and empty bowls lying filthy and overturned. Receiving food and water is the proverbial double-edged sword, as it is usually delivered late in the day and comes with an angry kick or two from a large boot, even though she lies motionless in a desperate attempt not to offend. On a few occasions, when her deprivation causes a momentary lapse of fear and she shows interest in the contents of the bowls, the booted monster will kick her back into submission. "*Please, don't move,*" I try to will her telepathically on days when I witness this cruelty.

Her people don't see fit to provide her with any shelter, so she has dug herself a hole in the dirt in an attempt to escape the elements. When it rains, she climbs out of the hole and lies next to it on the ground, head tucked tight under her leg. I constantly chronicle the dog's plight to my mother, who, like me, is both saddened and frustrated. "There must be something we can do for that poor thing," she laments one day as we pull out of my driveway.

"I don't have any idea what that would be, Mom."

On a hot summer day, after watching the neighbor's house for several hours, I decide the residents of what I have begun referring to as, "Hell House," are gone for the long holiday weekend. This is the first time I sneak over the property line and introduce myself to the dog. I walk through the length of my horse barn, through the attached expanse of my indoor riding arena and out the large sliding door that faces the west side of my property. I pause briefly at the invisible boundary of "ours" and "theirs" and take a deep breath before stepping forward to cross the twenty or thirty-foot gap between us. "How is this lovely creature today?" I ask her bending over and ruffling my hand on the top of her head while she lies motionless. "Mmmm," I hum to her, squatting down and caressing her chin now, "playing possum, I see. That's an interesting skill for a hound dog." I am somewhat surprised to see her name engraved on a brass collar tag. "It's nice to finally meet you, Sarah. My name is Laura. Not a news flash, but you have some shitty housekeeping humans," I pause to bend over and pick up a dirt-encrusted bowl. "Mind if I tidy up a bit?" I ask her conversationally. For both of our sakes, I do not let pity come calling with me. It will not bolster either one of us. From that day on we are friends. Every time the coast is clear, I bring her food, treats and fresh water.

In late summer, as I am pulling into my driveway which runs alongside the ramshackle house, I am mildly shocked and surprised to see the rare appearance of the old, toothless woman who lives in Hell House with her adult son. She is using the hose that is attached to the side of the house closest to my driveway to rinse off an undistinguishable item laying in the uncut grass. This is the break I have been waiting for. I quickly roll down the passenger side window and yell over to her in my high-pitched, fake friendly voice, "Hi, how are you?" I offer. My question vaporizes unanswered, and I am met with a brief, disinterested glance over the top of a lopsided pair of Dollar Store reading glasses. "Would it be okay if gave your beagle one of my old dog houses?" I ask in a slightly louder voice. I am trying to make my question sound casual, but it comes out slightly pleading. "I have one I'm not using anymore….".

I believe in the virtue of verbal integrity, but my belief is apparently not strong enough to stop this un-truth from rolling out of my mouth. Is the truth about the origin of the doghouse that is sitting inside my garage really that offensive? I believe, to these people, it would be. To them, it may appear to be a judgmental finger pointing; an insult, charity and an intrusion into their lifestyle, and it is all those things. When the woman mumbles something back to me, her lit cigarette bouncing in the corner of a mouth that resembles a piece of dehydrated fruit, I choose to believe she has given me permission. I park my truck and practically run to the garage, hit the door opener and drag out the brand new, state-of-the-art, insulated dog shelter my mother and I had purchased the previous week at the farm supply store. It has already been bedded inside with fresh straw.

I am damn near euphoric that the solitary beagle is getting a chance to feel the simple comfort of some cushion under her body and protection over her head. I drag my prize across the expanse of the yard cradling my cell phone on my shoulder.

"I'm taking the dog house over to the beagle," I announce breathlessly into the phone when my mom picks up."

"Oh my gosh, that wonderful," my mom says, "did they give you permission?" she asks sounding slightly disbelieving.

"I got permission from Satan's mother," I answer.

"Oh, Laura," is all my mother says in response to my insult.

At first the beagle tries to shy away from strange edifice plopped into her space, but she can only go so far on the short length of chain that's attached to a too-tight collar. "Easy, Sarah," I coo to her, "this is your new digs. You're movin' up from the dirt hole," I say enthusiastically. She sniffs at the dog house tentatively, but after a moment or two, she slinks in, circles twice and lies down. Her chain is just long enough to allow her inside. For a few days, I have a pleased sense of relief.

One evening not long after, while I am out in the horse barn doing the evening feeding, I hear the beagle let out a distressed yelp. I jog out of the end of the horse barn and look over at the space where she lives. Staggering across the yard carrying the dog house over his head is the drunken piece of human shit that holds her hostage. "Is there a problem?" I yell over, striding down to meet him at the chain link fence I had installed to clearly define the property lines. "Keep your shit out of my yard," he roars while hurling the plastic structure over the fence and onto our driveway. I hear the plastic crack on impact. He has already turned around, and while I am staring stunned and heartbroken at the dog house lying in the driveway like a broken egg, he slams his back door shut. I don't look over across the yard. I just can't. The intensity of my hatred for this man scares me, made worse by my husband's adamant demand that I mind my own business. "He doesn't give a flying shit what you or anyone else thinks about what he does with that damn dog. He's the type of asshole that will burn that goddam horse barn down if he thinks you're fucking with him. Let it go, Laura. I mean it!" And I do….. for a little while.

Hostage Negotiations

Despite my history with anxiety, I am reasonably comfortable on nights like tonight when Denny is out of town for a few days on business. There are sleeping dogs sprawled around the living room, and I am curled up in the corner of the couch watching HGTV. Several times tonight the dogs have picked up their heads, ears perked, and started barking in response to the loud voices they hear from the house next door. I walk into the darkened kitchen and watch out the window. Two teenage boys, who are frequent weekend visitors next door, are squirting what I presume to be lighter fluid on an already roaring fire not more than twenty feet from their backdoor. They are both jumping back, laughing, yelling and shoving each other toward the dancing flames. In the dusky light I can see the head asshole and another older, slovenly-looking man I had seen earlier in the evening. They are sitting in chairs on the opposite edge of the fire pit. Littered on the ground and illuminated by the flames, is a significant number of discarded beer cans. I watch for a while, willing the floating embers to land on the roof of their rental shack and send it up in flames.

"C'mon guys, last call for tonight," I say to the dogs. We all head to the back door and out into the fenced in back yard. I am standing still, patiently waiting for my charges to do their business. "Hey, go get that fuckin' dog," I hear one of the men slur, presumably a directive to the two teenage boys. My heart falls to my feet. "Why do you want the dog?" I whisper out loud. "Oh my God, oh my God, oh my God," I repeat frantically, scrambling back up the steps and into the house. I peer out the kitchen window just as the younger boy is handing his father the dog. I grab my cell phone but have no idea who to call. It is after 10:00pm, and my parents are sleeping. Denny is probably also asleep and would most likely be pissed off if I woke him up to tell him what has already been established: our neighbors are assholes. I'll call 911. I punch the numbers into my cell phone with trembling fingers, but I do not hit *Send*. I stand against the counter, chest heaving, and stare out the window.

When I make a move, I spin around so fast I practically fall over the top of my border collie who is never more than a few feet away from me. "Shit, sorry Buddy." I pat his side as I right myself. I yank open a kitchen drawer and make a frenzied search for a non-descript white envelope. My mom and I are the only two people who know it exists. We have set aside some money specifically for the neighbor's dog. We call it, "The Beagle Fund." We use it to purchase high quality dog food and lavish treats that I sneak over and give Sarah, usually in the early morning hours when I am out feeding horses, and no one is stirring next door. There is currently $100.00 cash inside which I snatch out and lay on the counter. I paw through the papers at the front of the drawer looking for a second envelope containing a bank deposit I compiled earlier in the evening. I quickly count off the $200.00 in cash resting on top, and discard the checks on the kitchen counter with the envelopes. The dogs are cautiously watching my frenzied movements. Shoving the cash into the pocket of my jeans, I head out the door.

"Hey guys," I blurt out, walking toward the chain-link fence, my heart clanging in my chest. "A friend of mine was over earlier in the week and he saw your beagle and was wondering if you were interested in selling her?"

"No," spits out Commander Shit-Head, who is currently holding onto the terrified dog, "She ain't for sale." And I stand, disbelieving, as he suspends her by her front legs and dangles her over the open flames of the fire.

"Oh, dear God, NO!" my voice screams in my head, but I remain mute. My intuition tells me that the dog will pay the price for my raw, unfettered hatred of this man.

"Catch," he directs to the oldest boy, swinging the dog across the flames that lick at her hind legs, butt and tucked up tail. She lets out a desperate yelp, and I think I see the fire make contact with her body as he heaves her, as hard as he can, toward his teenage son.

The kid catches her and briefly glances over at me. I stare at him in disbelief, silently pleading for him to protect her. He cannot, or will not, make eye contact with me. I wonder what I saw flash across his face the moment after he caught the dog, was it shame or fear? But, honestly, I don't care.

"How much will he give me for the dog?" the boy asks, still staring at the ground.

"The dog ain't for sale," slurs the drunken father who is sitting back down in his chair by the fire, cracking open a fresh beer.

"She's my dog," responds the boy softly. "How much?" he asks again.

"Three hundred dollars' cash," I spit out quickly and hold my breath.

"Right now?" the boy asks, briefly glancing up at me.

"Right now," I say, and pull the wad of cash from my pocket and hold it up in my hand like a bid number at an auction, for him to see. A few long moments pass, and I am silently praying. "Please God, please God, please God...."

His decision to walk toward me and lift the dog over the fence flabbergasts me. "Pussy," his dad growls and loudly sucks a wad of snot into his mouth and spits it on the ground. I stand on my tip toes and pull her over into my arms. As soon as the boy releases her, he grabs the cash from my still-raised hand and turns around to walk away. "Wait," I say quickly, balancing the weight of the beagle in my left arm while pulling a hastily written bill of sale and an ink pen from the right rear pocket of my jeans. My lengthy career of buying and selling horses has drilled into my head the need for proof of ownership. "Please sign this. It's a bill of sale. It says I paid you three hundred dollars to buy your beagle." When he hands the paper and pen back to me, I turn and practically run back to my house with Sarah bouncing in arms.

Once inside, I turn and deadbolt a door that hasn't been locked in over fifteen years and head straight for the stairs with my charge. The other dogs, curious and animated, follow me. They get their fill of checking out the newcomer while she lays across my lap, trembling so violently I can hear her teeth chatter. We sit on the bathroom floor next to the bathtub waiting for the warm water to work its way through the old farmhouse pipes. By the time Sarah is bathed and toweled dry, the other dogs have already lost interest and lie scattered and snoozing in the hall and bedroom. "I forgive you in advance if you go potty in the house," I tell her, cradling her in my arms and heading into the bedroom, "we're not going back outside tonight." When I walk into the bedroom, I call all the dogs to come in with me, and I shut the door and lock it. For the first time in my twenty-plus years of marriage to my police officer husband, I fish around in his sock drawer and pull out his personal weapon, a Glock .40 caliber, semi-automatic, and set it on the nightstand next to my side of the bed. "Holy fuck," I whisper, lying down in bed and pulling Sarah tight against my stomach, "I think we've both sufficiently had the crap scared out of us." She lies quietly, still trembling, under the blankets. "Tomorrow's a new day," I tell her, trying to relax. "Grandma Pat is gonna bawl her eyes out when she hears you've joined the family."

More Than Friends

The family has had their fill of food and everyone gathers again in the living room talking quietly while my father dozes in his recliner. "You're the last of the lucky ones, sister," I tell Sarah, stroking her head. And she is, in fact, the last in an unbelievably long line of souls that have found refuge under the love and comfort of my mother's protective wing. "You're gonna be fine girl......as fine as you can be when you're obese, smell bad and don't have a mom.......". "C'mon, let's go outside," I whisper down to her as I rise, stiff legged from the kitchen table.

When I head to the front door, grabbing a leash off of the small wooden table in the foyer, Sarah is on my heels. "Heading out with Sarah," I yell down the hall to no one in particular and pull the front door open. I stare at the dog as she wanders aimlessly around the yard and let the tears flow down my face.

When we walk back into the house, I unhook the leash from Sarah's collar, set it down on the table and quietly wander down the hallway toward my parents' bedroom, Sarah is padding softly behind me. At the threshold of the bedroom door I turn around, "No, Sarah," I say, pointing my finger down the hall, "go...don't follow me," I tell her in an angry whisper. She stands motionless, just staring up at me.

I turn around and continue through my parents' bedroom and into the attached large, tidy master bathroom. I flip the light switch on the wall and open the door to my immediate right.

One step and I disappear into my mother's walk-in closet and quietly close the door behind me. "Oh, my *God*, Mom," I am moaning, "this was a stupid fucking idea, Pat, leaving us here." I am stricken by a wave of sorrow so powerful that I am clutching the door frame to steady myself. I feel like I am going to vomit. "Breathe, breathe," I command myself and for a moment, I try my best to stand motionless until I can stop from gagging. Then, one step forward, and I am lost in a turbulent sea of sensations. My eyes are closed. I can smell her here, as if she is standing next to me. I wedge my body in between the row of sweaters that are hanging on the rack. I stretch my arms around as many pieces of her clothing as I can gather and bury my face in the fabric. I hang on to them as tightly as I can. I am squeezing my eyes shut, but that does not staunch the flow of tears. I try to trick myself into believing I am hugging my mother. My nose is lost in the faint scent of her body odor and the stale Calvin Klein "Escape" perfume that is lingering in her unwashed sweaters. But I do not fool myself. "I want one more hug from you, god dammit!" I am in agony.

"Laura?" I hear a knock on the bathroom door. "Laura, are you in here?" it's my sister entering the bathroom.

"What?" I mumble from the closet.

The door to my mother's closet slowly opens. "What are you doing in here?" Sorrow and pity have stripped away my sister's defensive edge.

"Come in and shut the door," I say. "If you stand over here and close your eyes, you can still smell her," I say sobbing. I move over and pull my sister next to me and demonstrate the sweater hug. When my sister and I finally emerge from the closet, I have tear streaked make-up and a pounding headache. Sarah is sitting just outside the door and follows us, unobtrusively, back to the gathering of our pack.

I have witnessed Sarah's suffering and chaperoned her away from the flames and fear that threatened to consume her. She is now returning the favor. In the weeks to come, Sarah and I will make this trek together, many times, down the hall, through the bedroom and into the walk-in closet of the master bathroom. I decide that Sarah and I have a soul sisters' song, Carol Kings, "Where You Lead," and I sit on the bathroom floor and hum it to her so she knows that someone still loves her. In return, Sarah will bolster me with her sympathetic brown eyes, stoic patience and unwavering loyalty while silently waiting for me outside the closet door while I cling to the lifeless sweaters and bawl my eyes out.

Courage

We gain strength, and courage, and confidence by each experience in which we really stop to look fear in the face...we must do that which we think we cannot.

~ Eleanor Roosevelt

Angel 2004

Fall seems to be the time of year Michiganders like the most. The crisp air, changing colors, football, apples, pumpkins, premature Christmas music and impending holiday time-off make people slightly giddy. It makes me slightly nauseous. Yesterday, as my mom and I sit idle in my driveway wrapping up another day of companionship and errand running she once again announces, "I just love this time of year!"

"I *know* you do, Mom," I answer with sarcastic resignation and an eye roll that makes her chuckle.

"You shouldn't be such a Scrooge, Laura," she says with mock scorn.

"I'm not a Scrooge, Mom," I say, tipping my head back against the headrest and batting my eyelashes at her, "Scrooge only hated Christmas. I hate all the holidays."

"Oh Laura, how can you say that? My mom sounds a little perturbed or maybe just disappointed.

Either way, I commence with a humming sound, my non-committal response to questions I don't want to answer or things I don't want to discuss. I give her a peck on the cheek as I climb out of her car.

"I love you Mrs. Claus." I say in a teasing tone, leaning back into the open car door "and I love the whole fall-themed sweatshirt thing you got going on there."

"I love you too, Scrooge!" she laughs back at me. My demeanor always softens at the sight of my mother's broad, genuine grin. It makes her eyes momentarily disappear under sagging, crinkled lids and exposes her golden dental work.

Today, I am on my own, but I'm doing my damndest to channel my mother's perpetual optimism on this drab November day.

"Don't…..move," I whisper to myself. I slowly exhale a shallow breath, and my body shivers slightly. I am attempting to stand motionless, but the rain-drenched leaves overhead are taking accurate aim at the exposed skin on the nape of my neck. I can feel the cool drops trickling down my back. I shiver again and grimace slightly from under my ball cap, but do not allow myself to make any sudden movement in response to the minor annoyance. I am dressed for the outdoor conditions, wearing a water-repellent, black, Eddie Bauer jacket, jeans and a ridiculously expensive, well-worn pair of ankle high, water-proof "barn boots" I ordered from a company in Australia. Not a frivolous purchase, I told myself, as I actually live and work on a horse farm. My denim jeans are damp and clinging to my legs below my knees, the result of my brief hike through the dense bush leading up to this spot, but the feeling is forgotten the second I re-focus my attention back to where I am standing. I have nothing against a rainy day, and on this particular morning, I am hoping it gives me a much-needed strategic advantage. I'm not sure that even my husband or daughter could compel me to be so persistent in getting my way. But a dog? Now that's a different story.

Where I am standing is only a few hundred feet away from the modern-day conveniences of paved roads, occupied homes and power lines, but with my back to the modern world, facing into the woods with nothing but brush, trees and a few dilapidated and long-forgotten structures in front of me, it is easy to feel isolated. I think back to the beginning of this quest. I would not have dreamed of venturing into these woods in the pre-dawn, rainy day darkness thirty days ago. But, I am braver now. Even so, I will progress no further until the sunrise, like the opening of a theatre curtain, illuminates the detail of the now-familiar scene in front of me.

I will not miss coming here every morning, but I have come to appreciate this spot. I understand now that it is something of a safe haven. I have stood here many mornings and studied this scape. There is a compelling, seemingly gentle blend of life and death here. The floor of the woods is carpeted with a mosaic of leaves that are decorated to celebrate the change of seasons. No longer sporting their vibrant, monochromatic hues of summer green, the increasingly colder nights are transforming them into free-falling, individual works of art, embellished in earthy jewel tones.

About thirty feet further on into the woods and slightly to the right of me, stand the remains of a once large and useful barn. Its presence here is the only indicator that this was at one time a place utilized by people. It looms now, faded and grey, with sections of its once-erect walls and weather tight roof gaping and partially collapsed. A carpet of ivy, also donning its darker autumn shades of deep green and burgundy, has emerged from the floor of the woods adhering unencumbered to what remains of the weathered walls. The entwined vines and foliage are so dense they look as though they are consoling the crumbling structure with a bear hug, gently covering the wounds that time and neglect have inflicted on it. I admire Mother Nature's endeavor to reclaim this space.

In a few short weeks, the remaining canopy of leaves on the tall ash and oak trees that loom overhead will be gone. The fallen leaves and brush will, no doubt, become brown and brittle with the increasingly colder temperatures, and fickle appearance of the sun. Sooner than I am ready for, this scene will likely will be dusted with snow.

A Rainy Day Break

The day begins as usual, when 5:15 a.m. is announced by the sound of chiming bells emanating softly from my phone alarm. My hand searches for the device on top of a tall stack of books on my nightstand. I am attempting to correct my blurry, middle-aged morning vision by squinting, as I disable the alarm, unplug the charging cord, and return the phone to its perch. "It's pouring," I say out loud.

My voice is like a magic incantation. It instantly brings the dogs in the room to life. My rule is, unless you have an emergency, like potty or puke, I get to make the first move. They are on their feet now and looking at me expectantly. I hit the ground running, as the saying goes, the daily reality of being responsible for the life quality of six dogs and twenty-two horses. My self-assigned role as care-giver to these few dozen souls, is a fact that propels me out of bed in the early morning hours 365 days a year.

"Yay for wet, muddy dogs," I mumble.

I extend my arms out, hands clenched into fists, and groan softly. I am allowing myself a luxurious moment to linger under the covers, back arched and body stretching with my eyes closed. I am listening to the rhythmic, muted thumping of heavy raindrops landing on the ledge of the window next to the bed. But the moment ends abruptly when the Chihuahua begins pawing persistently at the covers over my shoulder, and my right hand, resting slightly over the edge of the mattress, gets bumped and lifted by a damp nose. Not today, or any day, is this group interested in participating in a scene that looks like a Folgers Coffee commercial. They are animated and alert, prompting me, with their antics and tail wagging, to stop wasting precious, pre-breakfast seconds obviously awake but still in a horizontal position. I can say with absolute certainty, that there will be no aromatic scent of brewing coffee wafting into the bedroom to coax me down the stairs into a peaceful morning scene. For the dogs, the best part of waking up is having me as their servant.

I pull on my tired-looking 'Up North' sweatpants and equally tired looking men's grey, crew neck sweatshirt. I turn back around, patting down the rumpled bedding until I find the lump I am searching for.

"Come on, you lazy shit," I say with false exasperation.

I lean over the bed, shove my hands under the covers, and scoop out the toasty warm body of a handsome miniature pinscher. His name is Otis. We met on his "expiration date," my timing perfect for him, since he had just that morning caught an errant finger of a dog pound employee in his mouth. My best efforts to channel Perry Mason's cool and convincing defense tactics were successful, and the little black and tan bundle the workers had dubbed, "The Tasmanian Devil," was in my arms, a wide-eyed, angelic expression on his face, and heading home with me.

Otis groans his objections to being extracted from his cozy sleeping spot and cuddles into the crook of my neck. I rub my nose back and forth against his fur. I have always thought this boy smells like maple syrup.

I move down the stairs, dogs on my heels, flipping on lights in the hallway and kitchen. I make my way to the laundry room and lift the closure on the dog door.

"Go outside and go potty," is my daily morning command.

The three, large breed dogs, Rose, a Great Pyrenees; Kaya, a German Shepherd and Buddy, a Border Collie, blast through the dog door as I lift the panel that was inserted at bedtime the night before. They will go do their morning business and patrol the yard on high alert, looking for any potential changes since the closing of the dog door the night before.

Rose is the newest addition to our family and has been with us only a few months. We became acquainted at the Kentucky Horse Park in late summer. She was with a rescue agency, incognito as a homeless dog up for adoption. I was there with clients at a horse show posing as a dog- loving, do-gooder. Every morning I would pull up to their tent-covered staging area and pick her up. She would spend the day with me, riding around in my golf cart while I would tell everyone who took notice of her that she was available for adoption. One insightful stranger remarked, "Give it up, lady. She's found her person." And so she had.

Kaya, still referred to as "the puppy," is the resident adolescent. She has lived with us since my mother and I, on one of our weekly outings, spotted her and her rogue companion, a desperately thin and scraggly pointer, running aimlessly down a busy, four-lane road causing cars to swerve and horns to honk.

When my mom slammed on her brakes to avoid a collision, I jumped out of her still-moving car and gave chase. My mom followed, flashers flashing and window down, waving people to go around her. Tired and frightened, Kaya had responded to my somewhat demanding and desperate-sounding calls of, "Puppy come, puppy come," while her adult companion ran away from me as fast as his malnourished body could carry him. When I loaded her into the backseat of my mother's car I said, "Holy crap, mom! She's so flea infested, her coat looks like wheat blowing in the wind."

"Jesus, don't tell your father," my mother said, wearing an amused grin.

"Well, that's a switch," I say to her, and we are both laughing as we head toward the veterinary clinic to get the poor dog checked over.

Buddy is a moderate to severely neurotic Border Collie. I met him two years ago when a friend called to say that there was a dog running back and forth along the highway right-of-way fence. He claimed that he had tried to coax the dog to come to him, but his efforts were in vain.

"Nobody's getting near this dog," he said over the phone.

I could sense the frustration in his voice as he described what I would discover to be true Border Collie tactics. He would evade any type of pursuit but then always circle back, stop and watch.

We have literally just arrived home from vacation within the last hour. My husband, is basking in the reclaiming of his familiar bathroom space, and I yell up to him that I am running over to help "his buddy" with a dog issue. His parting words are, "Do not bring anything home!"

I leave the house in my non-pet-owning in-law's minivan and head over to check out the situation for myself. As I pull into the driveway of our friend's home, I can see the dog just beyond the house, on the highway side of the fence, scrutinizing my arrival. When our friend walks out of his garage to greet me, I jump out.

"Would you mind going into the house so he can't see you?" I asked, making a shooing motion with my hand.

"Um, I guess so," he responds, a slight look of rejection on his face.

"We already know he's not going to come to you. Don't take it personally," I say, the slightest hint of condescension in my voice.

"He's already surmised you're an asshole," I say under my breath as I watch him walk back through the open garage door and into the glassed-in breezeway of his home.

I open the passenger door of the van, and turn to face the dog as he continues to stare intently at me. I roll my tongue up in my mouth, lower lip tight against my teeth, and cut loose with a very loud whistle. The dog's entire body gets tall and stiff, ears perked and eyes fixed. He looks like a runner in the starting block, ready to blast forward when he hears the gun announce the start of the race. I whistle again.

"Come on, buddy," I command and make a sweeping gesture with my right hand. "Come," I repeat adamantly, returning his stare while making a quick, sideways nod with my head, "it's time to go home."

And to my surprise, he springs into action, running eight or ten feet down the fence line and wiggling his body through a hole. He never breaks stride as he dashes toward the van, jumps into the front seat and sits down.

"Well, then" I say, bursting out into surprised laughter while reaching in to ruffle the fur on the side of his neck, "it looks like you've been waiting for a ride," and I swing the van door shut.

"Holy shit! I can't believe that just happened," Our friend exclaims, shaking his head side to side as he walks out of the house. I actually can't believe it either, but I don't tell him that.

It is amusing when, a few days later, my owner search located his "people," and I discovered his call name actually was "Buddy".

Otis will also exit through the dog door, so he can dash around to the front of the house and bark unceasingly until I knock on the kitchen window and let him know his breakfast is served.

In good weather, Moses, the Chihuahua, also a death row dog pound resident, will make a show of exiting out the dog door if he knows I am watching him. He will stand directly on the other side of the flexible plastic panel until he hears me open the closet door to retrieve bowls and dog food. Once he thinks I'm busy, he hops right back in, walks past me like he's wearing Harry Potter's invisibility cloak, and proceeds into the kitchen to lift his leg and pee on the base of the kitchen table. When the weather is not ideal, like this rainy morning, he doesn't waste any time with false pretense and walks directly into the kitchen to relieve himself.

"It's like you're flipping me off first thing in the morning, Chi-chi," I tell him, using his more familiar nickname when he walks back in.

He is indifferent to my complaint and just blinks innocently at me with his bulging, black, chronically watery, old man eyes and then stares intently at the top of the washing machine while I'm mixing dog food. "I'm kind of in a hurry, you guys," I tell the dogs as they eat their morning meal.

I morph from my temporary status as food prep goddess back to a human peasant the moment the bowls hit the floor. Each dog progresses through it's morning meal at exactly the same pace as all of the meals, every day: no faster, no slower. The little boys I refer to as The Ten Pound Gang eat every meal like they've been deprived of food for days. Buddy is methodical. Like most of the tasks in his life, he approaches mealtime like it's a job, always eating his food clockwise in his bowl. Rose and Kaya are leisurely, Rose often looking up from her bowl to see where I am and what I am doing.

"You're absolutely right," I tell her when she looks over at me with one of her meaningful glances. I am standing, somewhat impatiently in the doorframe, "I will settle down."

The minute the bowls are empty and licked clean, I hustle out the door and into the dark where I am instantly bombarded by a chorus of "meows," compliments of the "porch cats." This demanding morning crew gathers daily and greets me with what sounds like a litany of complaints as they line up, single file, along the railing of the deck, to receive their portion of canned cat food. I take note that this morning, two of the older residents are absent, presumably still curled up and sleeping in their safe places in one of the barns.

I enter the horse barn through the door of the feed room. It is pitch black and quiet. The clatter of rain pounding down on the steel roof has made my entrance momentarily unnoticed. When I flip on the switch that illuminates the lights in the front section of stalls, I can hear several horses immediately respond with soft grunts and groans as they heave their bulky bodies up to a standing position and vigorously shake off sleep and sawdust bedding. Unlike their wild kin that are still acutely in tune with their flight animal instincts, my domesticated crew is laggardly in their rise to meet the day. A soft, sexy baritone greeting emanates from the stall closest to the door. Every morning I am greeted by this gelding's Barry White whinny. This big boy's sweet talk is easily one of my favorite sounds in the whole world, second only to my daughter's laughter. It is deep and rich. If luxurious brown velvet made a sound, this would be it. His name is Nick.

"Good morning you sweet, sweet boy," I lean toward the grill of his stall door and coo.

As I make my way down the row of stalls, several of the horses greet me with enthusiastic whinnies in the anticipation of receiving their morning meal. There is a large, red-coated gelding stabled about half way down the aisle on my right. As I come into his view, he immediately starts banging a front foot on his wooden stall door as if to say, "hurry up, woman, I want food now!"

"You could be the mascot for the brotherhood of athletic assholes." I mutter as I pass by.

I continue down the cement aisle way between the rows of stalls, "I gotta giddy-up today.......get it guys, giddy-up?"

I glance at the clock on the stove as I walk back into the house and hang up my damp coat. It has taken me a little less than an hour to feed all the animals. I am ahead of schedule by almost thirty minutes. There are no short-cuts in the routine, just me moving faster.

I dash upstairs to the bathroom to apply my make-up, which is my hard and fast rule whenever leaving my property, or prior to 8:00 am, whichever comes first. My intention is to be stealth today, so I will abstain from applying perfume, another tenet of my morning routine. Unlike most woman who repeatedly wear their signature scent, like my mother, for example, and her decades long loyalty to Calvin Klien "Escape," I refer to myself as a "perfume whore" and cherish the dozens of assorted bottles sitting on my shelf. I have, however, for the past twenty-nine days, applied the same fragrance: Vera Wang's Rock Princess, even on days when "Rock Princess," was definitely not representative of my mood. My goal has been to make my daily presence in the woods consistent and identifiable.

The use of a curling iron and firm-hold hairspray is my longest standing ritual, a habit still firmly in place with the passing of every decade. For a few years in what seems like my former life as an aerobics instructor and personal trainer I tried to break my dependency by getting bolder and bolder and having my hair cut shorter and shorter, but no amount of highlights and hair gel could keep me from purchasing smaller and smaller curling irons. In the end I just looked like a very fit lesbian……. or the Muppet character named Beaker.

These days I wear my hair in the stereotypical, Caucasian, middle-aged, woman's hair style; Short but not edgy; non-descript and just enough length to habitually tuck it behind my ear in my more animated moments. I try desperately to avoid the classic flat spot on the crown of my head worn by so many women my age. One can only assume that there is a tremendous shortage of hand-held mirrors in this country. I curl and spray my modest hairdo, sometimes multiple times in a day, and it lives on my head non-descript. That is, of course, unless I get caught in the rain at a horse show, and the combination of sprayed-on chemicals and sticky faux volume products has something of a shrinky-dink effect, and I end up wearing what looks exactly like Mrs. Potato Head's snap-on plastic hair. Today will be a baseball hat day.

I use my fingers to pull my baby-fine hair back into a ponytail. The result is a small sprig of hair projecting from the back of my head that is so short and sparse it looks like it belongs either on the head of a toddler or an aging hippie.

"Good enough," I announce, and the slumbering dogs snap to attention, and we all head back down the stairs. I open up the closet door and pull my black jacket off the hanger, slip it on and zip it up. I reach back into the closet and grab my recently purchased, hunter orange knit hat and pull it down over my baseball hat. On days when the weather has been hairdo worthy, I've walked through the woods twirling the fluorescent hat on my raised fist. "Hunter solidarity, man!"

My anticipated departure has Buddy and Kaya on to their feet and out into the laundry room, hoping that they will be invited to go for a ride.

"Sorry, guys, today this is still a solo run," I say, reaching down to pat them both.

Take a Deep Breath

"May my efforts today be divinely guided. I pray for the highest good." I rattle off my morning prayer while sitting in my truck, parked in its now usual location at the end of the neighboring driveway closest to the woods. "Today we leave together," I recite three times.

Somewhere along the way on my spiritual scavenger hunt, I had been taught to recite a prayer three times over if I wanted the Universe to acknowledge it, so this has become part of my practice. My words are part prayer, asking the Universe to support me in my endeavors and part manifestation exercise. The first step in bringing something into my life is to have a clear picture in my mind of what it is I want.

It feels important to have my quest come to a close today. I'm not sure I would be able to articulate why this morning is any different than the previous twenty-nine mornings I have ventured here, but I have had a "niggle" in my belly since waking up. I tell myself it is likely prompted by my less than enthusiastic feelings about the arrival of colder weather, coupled with the real dangers of entering this densely-wooded area during deer hunting season. Just yesterday, I had a cartoon vision of myself strapped to the front of an ATV with a guy in hunting gear yelling, "It's an old female, but she's got plenty of meat on her!"

The rain shows no sign of letting up. I pat down my pockets to make sure I haven't left any necessities behind and grab the white plastic grocery bag containing the usual items. Before hopping out, I reach across the center console to the passenger seat, grab the pair of leather work gloves laying there and slip them on. I shut the truck door as quietly as possible and walk to the edge of the driveway, checking both directions for signs of headlights, then jog across the road. I don't waste any time covering the remaining fifty feet or so of paved road before I make a hard left turn, step cautiously over the drainage ditch and into the woods. Today, I am hoping that my pre-dawn arrival and my now cautious, slow, steps through the woods in moderate to heavy rainfall will grant me the element of surprise. I have cleared my morning schedule of any time constraints and made a few key people aware of my early morning strategy.

"A month is long enough," I say to myself as I take a deep breath. In twenty-nine days, I have not quite mastered the ability to be completely at ease here. I will not miss this addition to my daily routine when I no longer feel obligated to come here. But even as I make my declaration, I know that if the outcome of today's visit is the same as yesterday's visit, I will come back again tomorrow.

If I Wasn't Supposed to Know, I Wouldn't

Twenty-nine days ago I was purchasing hay from "Curlers," a lady farmer who owns a large tract of land that runs parallel to this wooded lot. Her real name isn't Curlers, but my father's nickname for her has stuck. For a period of several months the previous spring and early summer, my father spent some time working with me when I was short on farm help. On the weekly trip to pick up hay, he would always ask me the lady farmer's name but could never remember it. I burst out laughing the first time he referenced her as "Curlers." It was completely accurate. She seemed to always have curlers in her hair with a bandana tied over the top. What made this even more delightful for me was my father resurrecting his long forgotten imitation of his favorite 1960's sitcom character, Gomer Pyle. I had grown up hearing my dad imitate the famous phrases from the TV show, but that silliness had been long forgotten.

Now, every time we arrived at her place, my dad would wait for her to appear, bouncing down the dirt lane from her house on her John Deere Gator and announce in his animated, ridiculous southern drawl, "Well, surprise, surprise, surprise, she's wearing curlers!" and we would both crack up.

And every time we pulled out, my dad would ask the same question, "Have you ever seen that woman without curlers in?" but he never waited for me to answer. The question was a set up.

"Gall-lee, I've *never* seen that woman without curlers," he'd say, shaking his head.

And that was the start of us calling her "Curlers." Every time I drive past her farm on my way into town, I always smile, thinking about my dad's laughter and antics, and how those few months that we spent working together on my farm are the best moments I ever remember spending with him.

Accompanying me on my hay run this morning is Craig, a man Curlers introduced me to the previous week. He had been doing some odd jobs around her place and is now working at our farm a few days a week.

"Hey, remember when I told you about that dog we had seen on the edge of our property a few times since way back in the start of summer?" Curlers asks him.

"Yep," is his brief response, but he continues to bob his head up and down several times even though he's done speaking.

"Well, my oldest son saw it early yesterday morning while he was tracking a deer. We thought maybe it belonged to someone around here 'cause we've been seeing it for a while, but he says it's living somewhere around the old barn up the road."

"Huh," my companion responds, accompanied by more head nodding.

"Whenever you're done dominating this conversation, I have a few questions," I joke, with my hands on my hips.

He throws his head back and lets out a single, "Ha!" followed by a show of raised palms, "by all means." He turns around and begins to effortlessly toss bales of hay into the bed of my truck.

"What kind of dog?" I ask her.

"Can't tell what it is. We never get close enough to really see it. My son says it's just skin and bones. Probably a Pit Bull somebody dumped off on the side of the road. He says if he gets a clean shot at it, he'll take care of it."

"Oh" I sigh, "that would suck…." I trail off.

"Well, we got little kids, dogs and farm animals here, we can't have stray dogs wandering around sick and diseased." Her response is quick and adamant.

My instinct is to counter just as quickly, "A dog that's been dumped by some heartless idiot and is starving to death isn't necessarily sick or diseased. It doesn't need a bullet, it needs help." The words bang around in my head, looking for the escape route out of my mouth, but I don't say a word out loud.

I pause to give myself a moment to decide how best to respond to her statement. She and I are both strong, sensitive energies. We are women who, at least on the outside, appear tough and independent. I refer to woman like us as, "high testosterone females." My husband is fond of saying that women like she and I can, "eat sawdust and shit out a 2 X 4," but the truth is, we are more like French bread, a coarse crust protecting soft insides.

Pausing, as opposed to blurting, is a recently discovered "tool" in my character development tool box. I'm still not very good at it. I have been diligently trying to apply this handy tool to all my interactions, but it can be tough when something resonates deeply with me. I am pleased with myself for my moment of silence, recognizing that this is exactly a situation where it would be both appropriate and beneficial.

A moment of quiet doesn't necessarily change what I want to say as much as it allows me to deliver my words less emotionally blunt and in a more relaxed and neutral tone. In this instance, it also allows Curlers a minute to smooth her mildly puffed up feathers, a visceral response in anticipation of defending her family's way of life. I know if I seem either confrontational or "silly," she will get mad, defensive, or will blow me off. Most farm folks I know, like this lady, who is the third generation to occupy this land, with both of her sons residing in the homes next door to hers, have a very familial and resolute way of looking at things. They are rarely interested in the opinions or suggestions of others. I doubt this dog is more than a blip on their radar--- a nuisance as they see it---and killing it would not be an emotional decision for them but a practical one, possibly even considered a humane act with the encroaching Michigan winter a few short weeks away.

"Tell him to give me a few days," I hear myself saying, trying to sound causal. "Let me see if I can catch it. I'll let you know if I have any success."

"Really?" Curlers looks bewildered and perhaps disapproving as I hand her the check to pay for my hay.

"Really," I smile at her. "I'll keep in touch on how it goes."

So this is the meaning of "Time Stands Still"

On my first night spent on this earth without my mother's physical presence here, I am lying face down on the bed. I am vaguely aware that at least three of my dogs are lying in the bedroom with me. Kaya, a small German Shepherd and the undisputed manager of my pack of six, is lying against the side of my body. Rose, a Great Pyrenees and the matriarch of the family, and Angel, an ancient Boxer, are lying on the floor next to me. My head is throbbing, and I am desperately wishing my husband would make the horrible sound in our bedroom STOP. Why, I wonder, are these damn dogs just lying here? Are all of you deaf? I have no idea what day or time it is. I sense my husband slowly lowering his weight on the bed to sit down beside me, and, when he gently lays his hand on my back and whispers, "shhhhh," I become aware, for the first time, that the sound is emanating from me. It is deep and mournful, so utterly bereft and desperate; I hadn't recognized it as human. The dogs follow my husband's lead. Kaya inches closer to me, gently licking the back of my arm, and Rose and Angel both stand up to rest their chins on the edge of the mattress by my head. Angel whimpers softly while licking at my closed fist.

This ensemble does its best to console me while my inner child is being amputated.

What I feel immediately following my mother's death is a raw form of acceptance. I share my day to day life with a menagerie of beasts: six dogs, twenty-two horses, ten cats and a mouse. Their needs keep me grounded. I lie awake in bed that first morning feeling vaguely ill and beat up. I am coming into this morning like most mornings, waking up a few minutes before the daily 5:15am alarm has a chance to sound. My eyes are thick and gritty, and my mouth is dry. I feel sore stomach muscles as I reach for my phone to pre-empt the noisy, unwanted intrusion of the alarm into this space. I never linger in bed. My husband says I would have made a great fire fighter, the way I hop up, get dressed and immediately start the day's "chores".

Normally, when my feet hit the floor, the dogs are up, animated with the anticipation of going outside to potty and devour the morning meal. This morning, however, they are awake but virtually motionless. My severe emotional hangover, with its warped energy, almost crippling headache and lethargic movements has them dubiously watching me as I struggle, blurry-eyed to put on the sweatshirt, sweatpants and socks lying in their usual spot at the end of the bed. "Thank you, guys," I mumble as I move past them in the still-darkened bedroom and head down the stairs to start my familiar routine. I am on auto pilot as I click on the light over the kitchen sink, lift the gate on the dog door and move to the closet to retrieve the stack of assorted-sized bowls. I am hoping my mind will sleep-in this morning, but as I measure out dog food and dump it into the dishes, the adage "life goes on" floats into my head.

Ready or Not, Here I Come

"Do you know where she's talking about the dog hiding?" I ask Craig once we are back in the cab of my truck and pulling out of the driveway.

"Yep," he answers, and I pause, waiting for more detail.

"And that would be?" I ask him, faking exasperation, both hands raised off the steering wheel.

"Just up the road, same side." He makes a pointing gesture back toward the direction that we came from.

I check for traffic and then pull out slowly, the weight of the hay making the bed of my truck creak.

"Do you mind if I stop?" I ask. My question is merely a formality because we don't know each other very well. Once we are better acquainted, he will know that I would stop regardless of his answer.

"Nope," he says, and I can see that he is enjoying my mild frustration with his sparse dialogue.

"You're a pain in the ass, aren't you?" I say with mock seriousness.

"It's what the wife says," he smiles, and once again his head is still bobbing after he is done speaking.

"Right up there," he says pointing to a clump of woods.

I pull my truck off the road as far as possible, but there is a drainage ditch just beyond the narrow gravel shoulder. I pull out the hazard light button and check in my large side mirror to make sure there is no traffic approaching before I open my door that will, due to the size of my giant, Ford dually truck and the narrowness of the available space, swing open into a traffic lane. As I jump out and close the door, I am feeling a little self-conscious about my large truck looking disabled, loaded with hay and precariously parked along the roadside in front of an uninhabited wood.

I stop in front of my truck, and Craig is sitting in the passenger seat staring at me.

"Are you coming?" I ask, gesturing as usual, arms held away from my sides, like my wishes should be obvious.

"Um, I guess I am," I hear him mumble as he climbs out of the truck and shrugs his shoulders.

We both negotiate the ditch, and in less than ten feet from the roadway we are in the woods.

"Do you know who owns this land?" I ask.

"Not a clue," he replies.

"Ever been arrested?" I ask.

"Nope," he replies.

I look over at him, "Have you ever knowingly trespassed on private property?"

"Nope."

"Well, then," I say walking deeper into the woods, smirking, "looks like this is our first memory in the making."

"Super," is all he says.

I stop walking when the barn comes into view and survey the surrounding area. Beyond where we are standing are a few smaller outbuildings. One is the remains of what was once a chicken coop, and the other I couldn't say for certain, maybe a workshop. It is square and looks only to be about ten by ten with basically no roof remaining. I am certain that a dog would not find shelter in either structure. Both are too exposed.

"He must have seen her in the big barn," I say and head in that direction.

"What makes you think the dog is a female?" asks my companion following close behind.

"Wow, a whole sentence just came out of your mouth," I say over my shoulder.

"Whatever," he says. His voice is tinged with a hint of annoyance.

I take a breath and soften, leaving out the sarcasm and answering with sincerity. "I think it's a female because of the amount of time that's passed." I pause at the threshold of the old barn doorway and face him. "She said they've seen this dog for months now. Something is holding her here. It obviously isn't food, but she's still alive, so she's tough and smart. Sounds like a girl to me."

I pause for a moment and peer back out into the woods. "No male I've ever met would sit tight in one spot for this long. Boys are needy. That's not a criticism, so don't be offended; it's an experience-based opinion." I turn and look at him with a wry smile on my face.

"If this dog was a male, he would be running cross-country, raiding trash cans and trying to find someone to take care of him, or he'd have been shmucked in the road by now," I say.

"That's very sexist," says my companion, chuckling, "and probably true!" His head is nodding again.

We walk single-file through the opening of the barn door. "This is bigger than it looks from the outside." I say, while cautiously moving a few feet into the interior of the old structure.

"Yep," I hear from behind me, "and breezier than it looks from out there," Says my companion, gesturing to the back corner. The thick underbrush and trees beyond the rear wall are in plain view.

"Complete with a skylight," I say pointing upwards to a large, open section in the roof.

Scattered around the floor are numerous old and rotten boards shed by the decaying roof. I take a few careful steps across the wooden flooring toward a section of half wall that spans maybe ten feet. The top rail of the wall reaches just above my knee. I carefully place both of my hands on it and lightly lean my weight forward. I am aware that there is likely nothing sturdy inside here anymore.

"That's where she's living," I say, gesturing with my chin toward the large, ancient straw mow that starts in the front corner of the barn. The top of the mow is approximately four or five feet higher than where we are standing and slopes gently down, approximately fifteen or twenty feet, ending abruptly at the wall. The straw mow, once a fluffy, sweet-smelling, golden expanse most likely harvested from a neighboring field and stored for cow bedding, is now a compressed, drab, grey-colored hill that smells damp and musty.

"You can see all the places where she's nested," I say, using my finger to point out several compacted divots.

"God, I hope she hasn't had puppies in here. I don't think it would have ended well."

The statement has left my mouth before I can stop it. This is another lifelong habit I am attempting to modify.

I grew up thinking that if my expectation was the worst possible scenario, I would either be proven right when it was horrible or pleasantly surprised when the proverbial, "other shoe," did not drop. Understanding my bad habits doesn't automatically make them go away. Making changes is a discipline, and the benefits are no different than yoga, meditation or working out. It requires constant practice, and the best results are accrued over time.

"I kinda thought maybe that's what we were walking into, that would explain why she's been here so long, but I don't see any evidence of puppies here….".

"Nope, I don't either," says my companion standing next to me.

"Hmm…..I'll have to give this some thought," I say. "Let's go get that load of hay off the truck."

We both turn to walk back toward the partially opened and sagging door that at one time would have swung smoothly on its large metal hinges.

As we step back out into the woods, my companion reaches out and touches my arm, "Over there," he says in a low voice and stands next to me pointing in the direction of the old chicken coop. We both freeze. I am scanning the scene in front of me for something that looks like a dog.

After a moment or two passes, I say in my normal voice, clearly frustrated, "I don't see anything."

"Right there," He leans in and extends his arm, finger pointed, into my field of vision. I am momentarily distracted by the smell of him. A pungent combination of cigarettes, horses and body odor. "She blends right in," he says, not moving, while I continue my visual search.

I slowly scan the area of low brush, and my heart takes a few fast, clanging beats when my eyes lock with hers. "I see her," I whisper quietly. For a long moment, the dog and I just stare at each other. "Hey, beautiful," I say in a low, friendly tone. She continues to watch us watching her, but the moment I move one foot forward in her direction, she immediately turns her back to us and walks away, disappearing into the overgrown brush. My companion and I make our way through the low brush, over to the area where we spotted her, but she is no longer visible.

"That is quite the disappearing act," I say, almost in awe of her ability to vaporize so completely. Her escape route is well planned out. After another moment of scanning the woods, I turn around and slowly start walking away, "Let's head back. She's gone for now." I say, feeling slightly deflated. After a few steps back toward the road, I throw my head back and yell, "I'm coming back here, girl. That's a promise!"

Thirty Days to a Better Me; No Money Back Guarantee

The following morning I wake up thinking about the dog in the woods, and my heart literally aches.

"I think we should all take a moment and thank our lucky stars," I say, glancing over my shoulder at the canine crew gathered around me while I prep the morning meal.

"Her life sucks right now," I sigh and go back to adding canned food into kibble.

I'm grateful for all of you…...even you, you little leg-lifting shit," I say, shaking a dog-food-covered fork at Moses, who responds with his signature watery-eyed, slow blink.

When my morning obligations to the animals at home are complete, I fill up a plastic zip-lock bag with a scoop of dry dog food, grab an unopened bottle of water, rummage through the "dog closet" for two extra bowls, and place these items in a plastic bag from the grocery store. I exit the house, closing the door on bewildered and disappointed dogs, and climb into the driver's seat of my truck. Moments after I turn the key over and the diesel engine is humming, Craig steps out from the end of the barn.

"I'm gonna go feed the dog," I yell out the open passenger side window.

He pauses for a minute, already in-tune to my idiosyncrasies, and yells, "Do you want me to ride along?"

"No, I think I'm O.K.," I yell back, and he waves a hand and walks back into the barn.

This situation requires action, I tell myself. Right action. My action. I close my eyes and envision the dog. I am already aware that she is close to starving. My source, Curlers, is unlikely to have embellished on that account. I also believe that because she evades human contact when it is available, it would be accurate to say she is frightened, possibly injured or both. She is, most likely, scavenging through garbage cans and eating road kill to survive. Despite what I believe to be her desperate plight, I know that interjecting myself into this situation emotionally charged and reckless would be detrimental to both of us. I will listen to my gut instincts.

I am sitting in the driver's seat of my truck alone. The radius of my "driving alone" comfort zone is small but encompasses most everything I usually need. The gas station, bank, post office and local market are just a few miles up the road, north of my home. Curlers' farm is located a few miles in the opposite direction, a route that is also familiar to me. Both routes are rural and devoid of heavy traffic, and in both cases, my destination is always somewhere familiar and with people I know. Rose, Kaya and Buddy are frequent passengers on most of my solo outings. Just the presence of these steadfast companions helps to keep me grounded. Because I am in pursuit of a dog, however, taking them with me this morning is not an option. A first encounter, possibly filled with fear, anxiety or protectiveness, is not a recipe for a calm introduction or positive first impression. On this trip, they will have to stay behind. In the few minutes I have been sitting here, I have already re-considered asking one of the farm workers to accompany me, but I quickly veto the idea. Every minute that they are away from the farm, the work is falling behind.

My vision of how this dog must be struggling to survive bolsters me against my own struggles. How ironic, I think, that this dog's situation is the exact situation I fear the most: being isolated, feeling insignificant, un-supported and possibly misunderstood. As I head out of my driveway and down the road, I feel the subtle mental shift that has me assessing my landmarks and available turn-around options, the hyper vigilant strategizing of an anxiety sufferer, and then I admonish myself.

"Oh for Pete sakes," I say out loud, sounding disgusted, "it's like two miles away." I press down the gas pedal, and as the truck leaps forward, I begin singing the only song that comes to mind, "This little light of mine, I'm gonna let it shine. This little light of mine, I'm gonna let it shine….."

I drive past the woods, pull into a neighboring driveway, turn around and double back. I park in the same spot as the day before. When I hop out of the truck, I grab the bag of doggie staples and head into the woods. The thick bed of dry, brown leaves announces every step I take. I notice my heart rate accelerate as I get closer to the old barn. I cautiously break the plane of the doorway, and I'm not sure if I am relieved or disappointed that my quick scan of the interior reveals that she is not inside. I have no doubt that my noisy arrival has provided her plenty of warning that there is an intruder into her otherwise quiet world. Dogs possess such acute hearing she was probably aware of my presence from the moment I slammed the truck door. While

I am walking toward the barn, she is, no doubt, walking away from it.

I decide to place the bowls directly inside the door to the right, up against the section of low wall. I look around and find two smaller pieces of scrap wood and place them on either side of the bowls to keep them from scooting around the smooth wood floor while she's eating and drinking. I pour in the bag of dog food and the bottle of water. I contemplate how nice it would be to bring her a big bone to chew on. That is my way. I am the mom that always brought extra costumes to the elementary school Halloween parade just in case a kid didn't have one. I do not have the heart or the stomach for involuntary ostracism.

But this girl doesn't need a bone, and while I definitely don't want her to suffer another moment of her life, I also know that making her comfortable in this setting would be a mistake. I will give her enough to survive, but there will be no extra goodies.

Pick This, Not That

I am the youngest in my family but the most outspoken. As a result, my mother and I had shared several intimate talks about death. On one of our outings, I had shared with her that my ideal funeral would consist of disposing of my body with a giant funeral pyre on the vacant lot next to my farm. I love the idea of all the elements coming together: the wood, the fire, and the sun, and not leaving behind anything that takes up space, just a pile of ashes for the wind to scatter or the rain to wash away. My mother laughed and called me "silly." She said she definitely wanted to be cremated too, no pyre necessary. She was content with the traditional method.

I remember this as my family travels in one car to the funeral home. My brother, sister, father and I are sitting in what I have dubbed in my mind after a brief walk around, "The Showroom of Death." We are perusing catalogues of caskets, being told what options and upgrades are available, and taking turns looking at the pictures, sort of like shopping for a new car. This room, whose décor is suspended in time, I decide, must have a secret airflow system that sucks all the emotion out so people can get through this process without a breakdown.

We are all seated around a large conference table acting as if we are participating in a board meeting, very matter of fact. We agree on an attractive, simple casket with no metal hardware, the burnable variety of course, as opposed to the more ornate options displayed in the "going to ground" section. We move on to the urn choices, and while we all agree it should stay simple -- she was not a flashy woman and would not appreciate a bedazzled resting place -- we tell our father he has the final say. We all like the green marble box. He agrees. On to the next decision. I have brought a current picture of my mom that was taken just a few weeks previous to her hasty exit, and, we all agree that it will be used for both the obituary in the newspaper and the memorial cards that will be handed out at the church the day of the funeral. We choose the Irish Blessing for the back of the cards. Her maiden name was Patricia Catherine Kirkpatrick.

We are gently prompted by the funeral director through the complete process. There are questions about visitation times, flowers, personal effects, family, out-of-town guests and pictures. Piece by piece, he is expertly and delicately choreographing our nightmare. When the question of music for the funeral arises, I recall for the group that on one of our trips to town, when the song titled "Celebrate Me Home," by Kenny Loggins was playing on the radio, I had said to mom, "I want this song played at my funeral." And after she had listened and hummed along, she had said, "Oh, I want that song, too!"

And so, my mom gets that song. It will be done in person by a local musician we all know, accompanied by his guitar. It is my father's adamant request that she also get a recorded playing of "Wind Beneath My Wings," by Bette Midler, which, as far as I'm concerned, is a song that I had hoped never to hear again after 1990. I do not strenuously object, only because it is his wife's funeral. So my mother gets a complete funeral package, her last big purchase, paid for by her life insurance policy.

Acceptance

Forgiveness is the fragrance that the violet
sheds on the heel that has crushed it.

~Mark Twain

Nona 2013

"Clearly you're some sort of royalty, or perhaps a High Priestess or Goddess," I say to her, as if I am stating the obvious. She doesn't respond, and we walk across the parking lot toward my truck in silence.

Her stride is long and purposeful, neither fast nor slow. Her posture is regal, head carried high with a composed expression on her face. I open up the back door of my truck and make a slight curtsy as she places a foot on the running board and effortlessly raises her lithe body onto the back seat. I stand by, patiently waiting for her to settle herself before closing the door. I walk around the front of my truck, open my door and toss my handful of paperwork up onto the dashboard before hauling myself into my seat, much less athletically than my passenger, and buckling my seatbelt.

"I absolutely understand if you don't want to talk about it," I assure her as I start the engine.

"I can see you've been through a lot," I sigh apologetically.

I think maybe I catch the slightest nod of her head, but I can't be sure. If there is any anxiety regarding our impending departure and the abrupt change in her living situation, it is imperceptible in her dark eyes. She is sitting quietly, gazing out the window.

"O.K.," I glance over my shoulder as I wait at the end of the drive for a break in the traffic, "I just want to tell you, you're safe now, and we'll do everything in our power to make you comfortable and happy," again nothing.

After a few minutes on the road, I steal a glimpse in the rearview mirror and catch her in a long, slow blink as her head nods slightly forward. Silently, I wish she would rest her head and allow herself to close her eyes and take a respite on the brief drive to the house, but she doesn't trust in that sort of luxury.

I park in my usual spot, turn the key off in the ignition and toss it in the cup holder. I unbuckle my seatbelt and twist my body sideways, wrapping my arm around the back of the passenger seat so I am now facing her.

"A few things before we walk in to the house," I say, resting my chin on my right shoulder, "I wasn't expecting company, so, I'm gonna make you a bed on the couch. I can arrange something more private if you need me to, but I think you'll be comfy. Also, it's a full house with a lot of personalities….." I trail off, not sure of what I'm trying to say, "We all do our best. I just want you to know that."

I open the backdoor of the truck, but she makes no move to climb out and join me. "I swear to you, this will not resemble any experience in your recent memory," or distant memory, I'm guessing.

"Come on, give us chance" I say, as reassuringly as possible.

She sticks her head out and watches the animated pack of dogs in the backyard. They sense, almost immediately, that I have not arrived back home alone. It looks like a synchronized dance scene as they gather, single file at the fence line, some, quietly lifting their noses upward to catch a whiff of an unfamiliar scent and others more interested in barking their greeting.

"C'mon, they're gonna love you," is the best thing I can come up with, but it seems to be enough. She steps down out of the truck and silently follows me up to the back door.

It is the usual mob scene when we cross the threshold.

"You gotta just walk in and claim your space" is my directive to every visitor, but she doesn't seem to need any advice from me.

Once inside the door, she pauses and stands patiently as pack members, some politely and some intrusively, touch and smell their way around her, gathering information that I will, most likely, never be privy to. After sixty-seconds or so tick past, I am confident she can hold her own.

"I need to go grab a clean blanket and run to the potty. Make yourself at home," I look over my shoulder for one more confirmation that she's fine where I leave her standing in the kitchen, still being investigated by moist noses.

I skip up the stairs, two at a time and quickly close the bathroom door behind me. I catch a glimpse of my face in the mirror with its slightly panicked expression.

"Holy shit I could kill somebody right now!" I am pacing back and forth across the bathroom floor, fists clenched and punching at the air.

I take a dramatic, deep breath, and blow it out forcefully with my cheeks puffed out. I lay my palms on the edge of the vanity and lean in close to the mirror so I am looking directly into my own face, blue eyes narrowed and teeth clenched.

"If I **ever** find the son of a bitch that wrapped a chain around that beautiful dog's neck and bolted her to a tree, I'll kill that hillbilly son-of a bitch with my bare hands." Tears are rolling down my face now, but I am not sad. I am pissed off.

"You human piece of shit: watching her, day in and day out, starving and freezing even *after* they warned you to feed her and give her shelter," I bend over and lay my head on my forearm.

"They had to cut her free for God sakes!" I am groaning and choking on my words. My breathing sounds like I just came in from a run.

I stay bent over for a minute or two. At first, my eyes are closed, but it is too easy to fill the dark space behind my lids with images of her suffering, so I open them and stare at the floor. I focus on the air moving in and out of my body, not trying to control it- that's a lost cause when I'm 'whipped-up,' but just witnessing the process as it slowly returns to normal. When I am more settled, I stand up, and once again address myself in the mirror.

"Ugh, get your shit together, woman." I reach over and tear off a section of toilet paper and wipe away the black streaks and speckles of my ruined mascara.

I grab a blanket out of the closet and head back downstairs. She is still standing in the kitchen, and her eyes lock with mine as I land off the last step. I shrug a little sheepishly.

"What can I say, I'm human, spiritually less evolved than you. I obviously lack your grace. Maybe you can work with me on that." I smile over at her.

I walk over, place the clean blanket on the end of the sofa, and she continues to stand, quietly composed, watching me with her charcoal black eyes. I think I can literally feel my heart melt when I look back at her standing there, a thoughtful expression on her face. I stroke her narrow, boney head while shaking mine, "I have no idea how a soul stays this lovely." She isn't contemplating her history; I know I shouldn't either.

"Alright, beautiful, let me give you the nickel tour," I tell her, and gently hook my index finger under her collar. Together we walk around the corner to the dog door.

"Allow me to demonstrate," I say, getting down on my hands and knees.

"Watch this," I say over my shoulder and climb awkwardly through the door, out onto the deck. Once through, I turn to face the opening and sit back, my butt resting on my heels and hold up the plastic drapes.

"Come on girl, there's sunshine and freedom out here."

She hesitates only briefly, as if to consider the best way to proceed, ducks her head down and easily passes through the opening. We walk down the stairs together, and I stand watching her as she ventures out into the grass and squats to pee. When she wanders back toward me, I realize that she's exhausted. We climb the stairs back up to the landing, but this time I turn the handle, and she follows me through the open door.

"Ok, technically you're my patient, and I say you need to get some rest now. This has been a busy morning."

We move as a pack into the living room, and there is no argument from her as I pat the clean, soft blanket lying on the end of couch. She lithely steps up, circles one time, and settles her emaciated body down. The other dogs sense my need to be with her. They gather close by, each one finding a place to lie down, but they are not intrusive.

"Good dogs," I praise the group in a low, quiet tone, "Such good dogs."

I notice that she barely weighs enough to make a dent in the blanket. I tentatively lower myself next to her and slowly stretch out, my thighs and torso spooning her.

"Is this going to be O.K. with you?" I ask her, my palm softly caressing her head and moving down the dull, brittle fur that covers her skeletal frame.

Her eyes are already closed. I lay next to her, propped up on my elbow, watching her body jerk slightly as she takes rapid, laborious breaths, a symptom of the pneumonia that had left her looking lifeless when a Sheriff's deputy had stopped to make a follow-up visit. The original complaint of a starving dog chained to a tree had been made ten days earlier. Because the owner had shown complete disregard for her life and the deputy's directive to take better care of her, he had cut the chain away from her neck, put her in his patrol car and driven her to the county dog pound.

I am staring at her face as her eyes blink open. I realize that my body has stiffened next to her. I need to reel my imagination in and stop fantasizing about a special hell for people who are abusers. I force a deep breath, relax my body against her and lay my head back down on my arm. Almost instantly her eyes are closed again, and her breathing slows. I marvel at her peacefulness. Despite what has been done to her, she has not brought her past with her into this moment. She inherently understands what I believe so many of us struggle with: that healing cannot take place where pity or anger resides.

There's No Such Thing as a Coincidence

"Laura, I got one in the back." I hear the county's veterinarian call after me as I head out the door.

I stop walking and after a brief moment turn around. Dr. M, as I call her, is walking toward me, rapidly closing the gap between us.

"She's not gonna make it here" she says shaking her head. "The sheriff's department brought her in this morning, an owner non-compliance case. She's been starved, shows signs of frostbite, and has a severe case of pneumonia. I can give you some meds," she continues, "but she may very well be past the point of no return. I don't know if you'd want to take on anything like that, but I thought I'd ask."

"Sure" I say. "I've got room. I'll take a run at her."

What I don't say is, I could feel the "niggle" in my gut the moment Dr. M called my name. Or maybe even sooner, like this morning when I woke up and decided to drive over here for a copy of a misplaced document. The true purpose of my visit is revealed!

"Let me have the girls get her checked out of the system. I'll gather up the meds and then have them bring her to you. She's pretty fragile so I'll leave her where she's at until she's processed and can walk out."

"Do I need to get her somewhere else?" I ask, "I can make an appointment while I'm waiting."

"I don't think so," says Dr. M. "She ate a few bites of food from the tech this morning when she came in. The pneumonia's the biggest hurdle she faces, and I'm not sure she has enough strength left in her to fight it. She's been fighting a long time."

"Ok," I sigh.

"Well, obviously it's not meant to end here or we wouldn't be having this conversation." My introspection vaporizes into the air. Dr. M has already turned her back to me and is walking away.

I am pleased that I have earned a level of respect and legitimacy with the people who work here. My conception and ultimate manifestation of starting a non-profit was born inside these walls. It began just a few weeks after the sudden death of my mother, when the Universe, in all its perfect wisdom, brought me here to stand at the end of a dog run containing a resident not only battered by life but forsaken as well. "Lesson number one," the Universe said to me, "look around, you're never the one in the worst shape. And lesson number two; you hold the power of transformation. It isn't magic, it's movement. Figure it out."

Witnessing suffering never gets easier. The sight of it awakens a part in my personality that I seem to have the least amount of control over. I feel deeply offended, horrified and have been known to rail incoherently (and profanely) about being forced to share a planet with vile human waste. But the Universe has been a patient teacher to me. Over the years, I have worked hard at being less emotionally charged and reactionary. Like making good food choices, this is often a grueling process. I have developed an awareness that these encounters are purposeful. This is not to say that suffering is acceptable, nor is it something we should not all be working toward resolving. I have simply learned that my offense or disbelief will not bring about resolution. I must act when action is called for or honor the process when it is not. My ultimate goal, simply put, is faith.

I snap out of a daydream when I hear the door to the tiny medical room open. Standing next to the technician is a solid black, female hound dog of some sort, identifiable only by the shape of her head and tail; the body is not representative of anything living. As the door closes, they walk toward me and the technician and I exchange pleasantries.

"These are her meds and paperwork. Instructions are on the labels. Dr. says to call if you have any questions, and let us know if she makes it."

"Will do" I reply, nodding my head and reaching for her things. "We're outta here, girl."

The Revival

Clearly she has already "made it" proven by the simple fact that she is here with me now and not lying dead, frozen and forgotten, bolted to a tree. I continue to lightly stroke her body. She has fallen into a deep sleep now, her breathing is a little slower, and she is snoring softly. She will continue to sleep for fifteen hours straight, and when she wakes up, I administer her medication, watch her eat and drink until she's had her fill and fit a warm polar fleece dog coat over her fragile, cool body.

I call her Nona. In the days following our meeting, she reveals her intention not only to survive her ordeal at the end of a chain, but to thrive. Her first signs of recovery begin with her spending more and more time awake. The deep shadow of fatigue and illness is slowly replaced by bright eyes and a less angular body. She blends in easily with the pack and maintains the same gentleness she exhibited the moment she entered our home. As her lungs heal, and her body slowly gains strength, I am touched to see her 'hound dog-ness' emerge.

Her manners are impeccable, which I find both baffling and extraordinary for a dog that has lived her life in the circumference of three feet of chain. Her first trips outside serve only the purpose of relieving herself, but as the days progress, she begins to venture out and join the pack in their daily ritual of numerous trips in and out of the dog door. The first time I see her standing stock still in the back yard, clad in her red sweater, eyes closed and nose lifted to the sky deciphering a scent that is floating in the breeze, I am in complete and utter awe of her grace. I step out the back door and watch her. She is only here, in the 'now', completely absorbed in the moment and fully content with herself. She has not carried the wounds of her past forward.

"I wish I could smell it with you," I tell her as I stroke the side of her long, hound dog nose and gently squeeze her ear. She rests her weight lightly against my thigh. "It looks like you're smelling heaven."

I smile and walk through the yard. The entire pack, including Nona, follows close behind. We are simply strolling, each of us enjoying the reprieve from the cool March air, the rays of sunshine and the glorious feel of the impending spring. Nona trots past me with the other dogs and joins them at the fence as they answer the call of the neighboring dogs.

"Woof!" she raises her nose and joins in the volley.

"Woof, woof," she repeats, looking pleased and content at the sound of her own voice.

"Thank you, Universe," I whisper into the wind.

The Reluctant Chaperone

As I sit on the floor in the vet's office, Nona is curled up in my lap. She is chubby and wearing her favorite red sweater. The coal black fur on her head is glistening under the florescent lighting. I feel sick to my stomach. I am staring at the wall contemplating the dichotomy of her situation. The years of cruelty and deprivation have caused her body structure irreparable damage. Her blooming body weight, coupled with her blissful joy at the ability to run and play with the other dogs has had a crippling effect on her. We have used several medications in an attempt to ease her discomfort, but I have watched her decline despite our best efforts. "Nona," I whisper, hugging her close to me, "I am not willing to watch you slide back into a dark place. You have mastered the art of acceptance; no malice toward anyone despite what you have been through." I close my eyes and lightly rest my forehead on the top of her head. "I'm honored to have been chosen by you. I will never forget the lesson on forgiveness," I tell her, the tears streaming freely now, "my humble gift back to you is the decision to liberate you from this painful, worn-out body."

The veterinarian, who had left us alone together to say our goodbyes, slides the door to the tiny exam room open and gives us an apologetic smile as she enters, a syringe of pink euthanasia solution held discreetly in the palm of her hand.

"Do you want to hold her?" she asks. I nod my head "yes" but I do not speak.

She joins us on the floor. "Do you want to leave her coat on? She asks.

"Yes," I nod my head. What I cannot say is that Nona loves her red sweater and is never happy when I take it off her so I can throw it in the washer. Even though I put another dog coat over her, I can tell she is relieved when her warm red sweater emerges from the dryer.

"You know how this goes, Laura," she says, looking me in the eyes. I nod my head again.

"I'm going to sedate her first so she just drifts off to sleep," she pauses, "and then I'm going to administer the euthanasia solution, and she will cross over peacefully. We'll be right here with her until she's gone." Even though this woman and I are great friends, I appreciate her gentle demeanor and professionalism in these tough emotional situations.

"Mom," I croak out as Dr. Margaret pulls out a small syringe I know is a tranquilizer from the pocket of her scrubs, "catch her for me, Mom…...and you….." I whisper into Nona's ear as she lies quietly in my arms, "give my mom a kiss for me, girl."

I close my eyes and recite the prayer of protection while gently patting her body:

"The light of God surrounds you. The love of God enfolds you. The power of God protects you, and the presence of God watches over you. Wherever you are, God is, and all is well, Amen."

Busted

I return to the woods the following day at the same time, and it plays out the same way. I walk in, and she has already walked out. I refill the empty bowls. They have both been licked so clean you would never know they were full twenty-four hours ago. By the third day it feels like a synchronized routine. I haven't caught sight of her since that first day, but I can feel her watching me. After re-filling her bowls with the same quantity of food and water, I turn and walk out of the barn. I pause a moment and scan the brush where we had spotted her the first day, but I don't see anything.

"Come on, girl" I yell into the woods, my body bent forward and clapping my hands as if she is standing in front of me.

"Come on, girl, let's go home, let's go home, sweetie," I say in a high-pitched, excited tone, but she does not show herself.

"Ok for you," I yell into the woods, "but you're missing out. I'm pretty wonderful."

I am chuckling to myself as I walk out of the woods and back to my truck, but I sober up quickly as I approach the edge of the road and see a man standing at the end of his driveway, arms folded on his chest and glaring unmistakably in my direction. Before I can preempt him he is shouting at me. "You're on private property. You can't be there."

"Hang on," I yell over and glance both ways before jogging across the road.

"I'm Laura," I thrust my hand out toward him, "I live around the corner on Henry Road." He is momentarily taken off guard with my directness. My guess is he has been watching me the past few days walking in and out of the woods with a grocery bag and is probably under the impression that I am operating a methamphetamine lab in the abandoned barn, not a far stretch for our rural area. The fact that I didn't jump into my truck and take off has left him uncertain.

He tentatively shakes my hand. "That's private property," he says again, thrusting out his chin in the direction of the woods, "I keep an eye on it for the owner."

I'm guessing that's a self-appointed position. I keep that thought to myself.

"There's a dog that's taken up residence in the old barn," I say. "I buy hay down the road, and they told me about her. I'm trying to catch her before she gets shot by a deer hunter, or Animal Control gets wind of it."

His demeanor instantly changes, and his whole expression brightens. "I've seen it a few times, once or twice, always right around dark. It will come out and stand at the edge of the road and start barking. When I walked down the drive, it hustles back into the woods. Seems kinda sad," he says, staring momentarily at nothing on the ground, his brow furrowed.

"I think it's sad too," I nod my head in agreement. "I'd like to get her out without a lot of fanfare. I don't want her to end up like the dog at the airport with every idiot in the county chasing it, and then the authorities having to shoot it because it's so terrified it is deemed aggressive." I make the quotation mark gesture.

"No, no, I understand," he says. "I wish you luck. Why don't you park in my driveway? That's not safe out in the road," he gestures toward my oversized dually truck. "Stick to the left side so we can get in and out," and he turns and points in case I am not clear on what he means by 'left side.'

"I'm surprised the Sheriff's Department hasn't stopped yet to check you out," he continues.

"The parking spot would be awesome, thank you so much," I say and offer my hand again to shake his, "and thanks for not calling the cops on me." I can't help but smile when he looks a little sheepish.

Purpose

*Compassion is not a relationship between the healer
and the wounded. It is a relationship between
equals. Only when we know our own darkness well,
can we be present with the darkness of others.*

~ Pema Chodrin

Louie 2011

"I'm not sure you're gonna like how this ends," my husband Denny says from the passenger seat of my truck. These are the first words spoken since we climbed in, after I ended my conversation with the veterinarian several minutes ago. We have been riding in contemplative silence, heading north on the highway. I don't respond to his statement right away, and the quiet is interrupted when my phone rings again. It is our local veterinarian, Dr. Tim. He is also returning my Saturday afternoon "S.O.S." I tell him I appreciate his return call, but we are already headed to the vet's office in Lansing. Dr. Margaret returned my call first and is waiting for us at her clinic. Dr. Tim would have been equally helpful in this situation, but I am certain he is not disappointed that he will not have to return to the clinic after hours on the weekend. We are five minutes into our thirty-minute drive. I know the dog in the backseat will not die in my truck; he is sitting, chin propped between the headrests and nose pressed against the cool window, watching the world whiz past. But as my husband has already implied, ultimately he may not survive either.

My husband's statement is hanging in the truck like one of his farts, potentially offensive depending on my mood, harmless but waiting to be acknowledged. "Well.....if he's gonna die," I pause, "at least I know now that it's not going to be a long, drawn out, agonizing death, laying on a cold cement slab, broken and forgotten." My tone is slightly clipped. "If a humane death is the best I can offer him at this point, I'm good with that."

I have to make a concerted effort not to let my frustration with the situation cause friction between the two of us. We often champion the same cause but more often than not from two completely different perspectives. I wonder if other couples fight like we do: on the same side of the fence, passionately arguing the same exact point in two different languages, me in womaneese, and him in maneese. I guess it's just semantics. I know in this case my husband's motive is not to seem callused, but his lifetime in law enforcement is reflected in his response to this type of emotionally tense situation. He takes the worst case scenario and works his way backwards. In the early days of our marriage, his very convincing scenario-painting coupled with my vivid imagination and my first-hand knowledge that it is possible, without any warning, to end up in a scary place, had been like stoking the coals of my emotional meltdown.

The post-meltdown me takes a lot more responsibility for myself. It took some time to figure it out, but my life is about me. I have not discovered anything unprecedented but have come to realize what so many know----and so many don't know: how I process my life experiences is completely under my control. That's not to say that I have life figured out; it simply means I don't let a day pass without doing some type of spiritual homework. I am a seeker of personal peace.

My husband thinks he is a realist, and I am a dreamer. I think I am an optimist, and he is a catastrophizer. Either way, we've been pulling off this balancing act for almost twenty-five years now. So we must both be right, at least for each other.

"Why in the hell do they leave a dog in this condition alive and suffering?" He nods his head toward our silent passenger in the backseat.

"I have no idea what their motive was. He's obviously been someone's pet. He's neutered and has had his dewclaws removed. Maybe they were hoping the owners would show up," I shrug, feeling slightly self-conscious that we are discussing him like he can't hear us. He may not be processing the words, but I know he knows that we are talking about him, and he is definitely processing our feelings.

"Well, Jesus Christ, like you said, they fucking charge people for animal cruelty, and they leave something like this laying in their facility in plain view!" he laments, throwing his hands in the air, "What the hell?!"

He's on board, I think to myself looking over at my exasperated husband. This dog's plight has already touched him. Wherever this situation is going, he's already on board. Whatever this dog and I need, my husband will be there to help us.

We started out on this cold, sunny February morning traveling this exact same route, driving forty minutes to the Ford dealership where we purchased our truck to take advantage of our complimentary oil change, the perk for purchasing a truck that cost almost twice as much as our first home. While I am cooling my heels in the dealership lounge (I suck at doing nothing), I get a call from the woman who works the front desk at the county dog pound.

She has gotten permission from someone higher up on the "food chain" of our local, county government-run agency to hand me the dog after hours today, if I'm still interested.

"Absolutely, what time do you close?" I ask, walking over to the giant glass window next to the service department, willing my truck to materialize.

"I lock the door at noon," she says, very matter of fact, "and I have to be somewhere, so I won't be able to wait." She has made it perfectly clear: my window of opportunity is open just a crack (and in her mind she is the granter of the gift), and if I don't squeeze through it and back out before it closes, I will not be offered this chance again. If it doesn't go my way, it won't be because she didn't do her part; it will be because I failed. It's an interesting human tendency: people make it abundantly clear that they have the upper hand, even when it's completely irrelevant or, more to the point, unnecessary.

This dog drama I am immersed in starts innocently enough when one of my "niggles" leads me to stop in at the county dog pound. While walking down a row of cement and chain link runs, I stop and stare at the sleeping figure of an emaciated, buttercup yellow, purebred Labrador. I squat down in front of the run and grab the chain link with both hands. "Hey, buddy, what's your story, huh?" But he doesn't move. He is lying on his left side lengthwise in the run, head towards the door and butt towards the back, facing the sidewall. I scrutinize him a little closer, staring at his abdomen to confirm that he is breathing, "Jesus, buddy, you're super skinny." He couldn't be more still if he was dead. I slowly reach up and slide the latch that locks the door to the enclosure. There is a loud clang when metal meets metal, and it echoes inside this cavernous structure. I pause for a minute. I'm not sure why, but I'm holding my breath waiting to see if the noise will prompt an employee to walk back and investigate, but no one appears.

What I don't realize in those first few moments of my scrutiny is that what I am seeing will have a profound and lasting effect on me. The dog slides his nose back across the cement three or four inches so that he can see me. I am met with a pair of chocolate brown eyes so full of pain and sorrow it literally takes my breath away. He appears completely defenseless and at my mercy. I am prone to crying, but what I see in his eyes is so blatantly desperate and heartbreaking, I do not tear-up as usual. I am momentarily overwhelmed. He is literally begging me to help him. I can feel my heart thumping in my chest. We gaze unwaveringly into each other's eyes. My momentary emotional paralysis is quickly replaced by one of my more common tendencies, the vigorous use of profanity.

"Holy shit, buddy, what the *hell* is going on here?" In response to my question, I receive a slow, almost imperceptible, shift of his tail, his very Labrador-esque attempt to acknowledge my presence.

"Dude, is your back broken? Surely, they wouldn't leave you laying here if that was the case," I say incredulously. Still crouched down, I open the door to the run wide enough to accommodate my body. My right hand is still grasping the door, and I use my left hand to pat the top of my thigh. "Come here, buddy, come here," I say to him in an animated voice. "Come on, come here and see me," I prompt him again. I sound manic, but it appears to be working: his tail is sliding again, slowly, and only an inch or so, back and forth across the concrete. "That's a good boy" I coo, "he's a good, good boy. Come here and see me." With an effort that appears too strenuous for his frail, undernourished body, he rolls himself up on to his chest. "Oh, that's a good boy," I encourage him, still patting my thigh, "Come here, come on, buddy." He pauses, and for a moment he glances down at the floor and then back at me. He is mustering every ounce of strength he has in an attempt to fulfill my request. "Come on, sweet boy, you can do this. You gotta help me out so I can help you out." My voice is serious now, "Come on buttercup, get your ass off that floor." And, miraculously, he does. With another tremendous effort, he hauls his body upright and is standing in front of me, feeble and wobbly on three legs. I shift my weight to look at the right side of his body. From his very exposed ribcage to his tail there is virtually no structure, just a leg dangling uselessly from the area where a hip should be but isn't. He looks like a stuffed animal that's had all the stuffing pulled out.

"What the fuck happened to you?" I ask him solemnly, almost under my breath. "Geez, you look like a partially deflated dog balloon," I tell him as I reach toward him and cup his chin in my hand. In response to my touch, he closes his mournful, brown eyes and rests the weight of his head in the palm of my hand. This gesture has me reeling. His wordless desperation is pulsing through my body. "Dear God," I mumble, dropping to my knees and kneeling down in front of him. I use both hands to caress his velvety soft ears. With complete disregard for the hygiene of our setting, I lean in and kiss the top of his head. "You're a very brave boy," I tell him. "I'm gonna go see how to get you out of this. You gotta hang in there, buddy. Can you do that for me?" I lift his chin up, and he gives me a doleful look. I lean forward and plant another kiss, this one on the end of his warm, dry nose. When I pull away from him and stand up, I take notice of the untouched bowls of food and water. I do not look back at him, but when metal bangs metal as I close the door and the latch slides in place, my heart aches in my chest. He is once again isolated and alone, his spirit and body both broken, "but not forgotten, not anymore," I say under my breath, shaking my head. There is a card attached to the door that lists some basic information: his breed, sex, approximate age and general location he was reported to be found in. I'm only interested in one thing, what was his arrival date at the shelter? *Ten days*. The card says this dog has been laying in here for ten, misery-filled days. It does not say he is available for adoption. I have an elevated heart rate.

As I walk down the hallway and back to the front desk, I remind myself of the pitfalls of what I refer to as "emotional aerobics," a tendency to come at a situation too strong, too opinionated, or most often in my case, too blunt. I know when I am met by other people's emotional aerobics one of two things happens: I rise to their level of dramatic unproductiveness, or I shut them out.

"Hey, what can I do for the yellow lab back there?" I am hoping I sound way more relaxed than I am feeling.

This situation requires diplomacy. My previous experience with several of the employees of this local, government-run agency has taught me that. I sense a high degree of apathy and burn-out here, but I have no doubt that it is directly related to the number of knuckle-heads and bullies these workers are exposed to on a daily basis. Empathy seems to be a largely missing ingredient, but I imagine it's the only way they can survive inside the walls of an animal facility like this one where death is routine. For the majority of the animals that end up here, their only offense is that they have been discarded or abandoned and are ultimately unwanted. I wouldn't last a day working here.

"What do ya mean?" she asks distractedly, her eyebrows raised as she taps away on the keyboard in front of her. The phone to her left is ringing incessantly, but she doesn't appear to notice.

I respond with a closed mouth smile. The "Little Me," commonly called the ego, is present, alert and is making a valiant effort to pry my mouth open to render a descriptive and emotional overview of what I have witnessed not fifty feet away from where we are having this conversation, preferably with big, animated hand gestures. The "Big Me," knows if I take the bait and respond to her diligently practiced aloofness, I will get nowhere on behalf of the yellow dog. I smooth my own hackles with a deep breath; I fight the urge to sigh and shake my head. *Just have an honest fucking conversation with me,* I want to scream at the top of my lungs. *This isn't about you or me for God sakes, we can end his suffering. Why is it so fucking important to you to make sure I understand I'm insignificant? Aaaaaaaagh!!!!* The "Little Me" insists on airing its grievances. I'm grateful that the "Big Me" at least manages to hit the mute button.

"I'd like to help, and I think he needs it," I say with sincerity.

"I think Doc has him on pain meds," she replies, pausing her movement on the keyboard and at least glancing at me.

"Oh, I'm sure he's been triaged," I say brightly, overemphasizing that I *am not* implying anyone here has dropped the ball, "but he looks like he needs some extensive medical care, possibly beyond the scope of a once a week contract vet with a jam-packed spay and neuter schedule." I take a necessary pause to stuff an imaginary sock in "Little Me's" mouth............"He looks very sad and broken," I say with a frown, "I'll take complete financial responsibility. I can't imagine the county saying *no* to that."

"Let me see what I can find out, and I'll get back to you," she sighs. "What's your number?" she adds, shuffling papers on her desk, looking for something to write on. "Go ahead." I recite my number, and she writes it down followed by direct eye contact and a tight-lipped, dismissive smile that fades like a chalk drawing in a rainstorm when I don't make a move to leave.

Uh, oh.......	"Big Me" and "Little Me" are joining forces, I am currently a blend of purpose laced with impatience. "Ya know," I say, a grimace on my face implying that it pains me to speak the following words, "This agency is supposed to enforce animal rights, and, well, despite all the good things you guys do here, and regardless of what's been done for that yellow dog, I think the length of that dog's stay here and his tragic physical condition could be construed as inhumane.......". It is my turn to raise my eyebrows. I look around to make sure the coast is clear, and then I play my trump card.

"Do you think I should just call the Sheriff and ask him if I can remove the dog for medical treatment?" I ask the question, eyes narrowed, leaning on the counter, conspiratorially toward her. She freezes. The mention of me taking this situation outside of the confines of this building and this group of people has momentarily knocked her off balance. I can see her hackles are up now.

My husband says it has always been this way with Animal Control. It is viewed as the "bastard child" of county government. A necessary evil in every community, he says, always a political hot potato wrought with controversy and management issues. I know the overseer for this agency has changed several times, and it is currently under the direction of the Office of the Sheriff.

A few years ago I worked tirelessly and very closely for several months with this agency assisting in a large-scale horse abuse case. Many of the employees involved in that effort are no longer employed here. Although never appearing blatantly obvious, I know that there can be great heart in this collective. Unfortunately, it can be hard to glimpse hiding behind their shared defensiveness. This facility is under constant scrutiny and criticism from the community, yet its existence is necessary because of the same community. There is a pervasive mentality here of Us (animal control) vs Them (everyone else). The "Them," on the left side are viewed as the ignorant, irresponsible and misinformed public, and the "Them" on the right side are viewed as ignorant, arrogant, micro-managing administration.

This agency has recently undergone some significant changes, starting with the retirement of a burned-out director and the recent acquisition and move to this newer, more modern facility. The former shelter was a dismal and disheartening venue for both man and beast. Yes, they are undergoing big changes here, and I am hoping that the dramatic improvement in working conditions will effect positive change in the staff.

Because she knows I actually do have a legitimate, close connection to the law enforcement Kingpin of the county via my husband, she composes herself and instantly morphs into my ally, at least to my face. I realize I am running the risk of someone getting offended. I know a few of the players here, and it is not outside the realm of possibility that they may feel compelled to make it clear to me that the decisions regarding animal care are none of my business and euthanize the yellow dog in spite of my offer. That's a risk I'm willing to take and based on his condition, not necessarily a tragic conclusion.

All the Kings Horses and All the Kings Men............. Get a Second Chance

"Holy cow, I can't thank you enough," I tell the front-desk dog pound sentry. "I really appreciate your help with this. You're amazing! I'm in Lansing getting the oil changed in my truck, but it should be done any minute, and I'll head straight to you."

As if to test my resolve, ten miles into the trip back on the highway, we drive directly into a white-out. Huge snowflakes are blowing and swirling around the truck in a dense curtain of white confetti. I know some people think of such occurrences as a "sign" that maybe something isn't supposed to transpire. On the other hand, I interpret this temporary impediment as a test of my resolve, a chance to prove myself worthy of being the yellow dog's guardian. My speedometer is holding steady at 40 mph, and I have both hands clamped on the wheel. My husband's long ago warning to our youngest daughter after she planted her car in a snowbank resonates in my head, "You can't arrive in all your fabulousness if you're dead." She was appalled at his frankness, but, like me, I doubt she has ever forgotten the warning. The memory makes me smile.

"What are you smiling about?" my husband asks me, looking over from the passenger seat.

"Just life," I answer back.

"So, I gotta ask ya, why are we beating feet back to Jackson to get a dog we don't need? He doesn't try to hide his annoyance. *This isn't about me needing a dog,* I think to myself. "I doubt very few people, with the exception of the disabled, actually ever *need* a dog, Denny. I think dogs are usually in the 'want' category."

"Ok, why do you *want* this dog?" he asks smugly.

Denny is unaware of the dog's tragic circumstances. I have kept that to myself so that if my efforts to free him from Dog Hell do not succeed, I will not be exposed as a failure.

"Weeeeeell," I grimace and look over at him, "He's actually a very broken dog. Remember how Wile E. Coyote always ended up squashed on the pavement after his failed attempts to drop a ten-thousand-pound Acme weight on Roadrunner? Well, that what this dog looks like. Only it wasn't the Roadrunner that bested him; it was a car.

My husband is silent for a moment, staring straight ahead out the window. "Who's gonna pay for this?" he finally asks in a quiet, flat tone.

"Don't worry, *you* won't be paying for any of it," I answer back forcefully.

"What makes you think you can afford it?" He is working hard at trying to sound non-confrontational, but it comes out as condescending. The tension is as thick and stifling as August humidity.

Oh, you pious, son-of-a-bitch,' I think to myself. *'I'm familiar with this routine: you're the calm, steady voice of reason, and I'm the manic, flighty, do-gooder that hasn't thought this through...... well you can kiss my ass you non-visionary pain in the neck! Huh, talking to me like a priest in a confessional. Whatever!!!!!!* I take a very, very deep breath.

Twelve months ago, we would not have been having this conversation. Twelve months ago my mom was alive. She has always been my enthusiastic and generous co-conspirator in my animal escapades from as far back as I can remember. Denny has always been more of a bystander, a frequently pissed-off bystander.

"I'm not worried about how I'm going to pay for it, and I'd appreciate it if you wouldn't worry about that right now, either."

We are surely both reflecting on the absence of my mother. Neither one of us is sure how to navigate through this discord. I miss my mother every day, but the fact that she is not here with me now, laughing and crying over the fate of the buttercup yellow dog, makes the hole in my heart feel like a gaping wound. She and I always just jumped in, heart first. I am way out of my element trying to have a pragmatic discussion with my husband about what is compelling me to help this dog. I resent his acting like such a man.

"What's happening to this dog, Denny, is wrong on so many levels," I say, and continue to share with him my Thursday visit to the dog pound. This tricky emotional footing has me feeling fatigued. My anger softens into sadness.

"I honestly thought when I threw down the neglect card," my eyes are brimming with tears now, "he would disappear. That's obviously not what happened......." I trail off. "But now that I'm aware of him, I can't pretend he doesn't exist. I can't pretend that I don't think the Universe showed him to me for a reason..........I have no idea why I'm crying," I say, frustrated, attempting to swipe tears away from my eyes before they run down my face and streak my make-up.

"Yes, you do," my husband says, with the sigh of gentle resignation, "Let's go pick up the fucking dog."

My Big Girl Pants Must have Shrunk in the Dryer

It is Thursday morning, and I have spent the last ten minutes wandering aimlessly around the kitchen, opening and closing cupboard doors, shuffling junk mail on the kitchen table, and now I am standing, arms outstretched, freezer door handle in one hand, and refrigerator door handle in the other, staring intently at the contents inside. What I need at this moment doesn't exist inside the bowels of an appliance, even though, "food for thought" has been a literal motto for me most of my adult life. On occasions too numerous to count, I have contemplated the complexities of my life over a box of Entemen's chocolate-frosted doughnuts or an entire bag of candy. But at this mid-life stage, I can say with absolute conviction that if wisdom and personal growth could be found in a pastry box or a king-sized bag of frozen, peanut M&M's, I'd have won a Nobel Prize by now.

I need to go over and feed the dog. The bag of dog food and bottle of water have been re-loaded and are setting on the end of the kitchen counter, but I am frustrated with myself. My ego is an impatient and unsympathetic mediator this morning between my physical self and my emotional self.

"Put your big girl panties on." I say out loud as I climb into my truck. But even as the scornful words come out of my mouth, I know that berating myself is both futile and ineffective. I am, at the moment, looking at myself the way many people look at anxiety sufferers: with impatience, annoyance and judgment. I am already aware that I cannot bully myself into better emotional health, but on some days, old habits die hard. I am fidgeting again, arranging my phone on the console and looking through my purse for sunglasses that I don't need this time of the day. I reach over and press the radio on, and my truck is instantly filled with James Blunt crooning, "You're beautiful, it's true."

"Oh, shut up, James!" I say, glaring at the offending radio and punch the button that will silence him.

I back my truck out along the front of the garage and then pull forward to the end of the driveway. After checking both directions, I press on the accelerator, but instead of turning right and heading to the old barn, at the last minute I awkwardly turn my truck to the left. I go about a hundred feet and turn back into the second driveway on my property and circle around, almost to the point where I started. My truck is at a standstill, but my heartbeat is accelerated and the palms of my hands are lightly sweaty. I grab for my phone and dial.

"Hello, Laura," my father answers the phone sounding wide-awake and business-like despite the early morning hour.

He and I are both early risers. For the past several years, after an exchange of pleasantries, his first remark was a question; "What time did you get up this morning?"

It was something of a contest to see which of us had gotten up the earliest, and he was certain it was him. I have spent a significant part of my early adult life trying to override my feelings of inadequacy regarding my lack of collegiate education with an overcommitted schedule and lack of sleep. But with the passing of time, my father's full retirement and his increasingly intimate relationship with his nightly bourbon, the relevance of the question no longer matters to him. I have finally won the insignificant family title of "Wake-Up Champion."

"Hi, Dad, I need to talk to Mom," is all I say.

"It's Laura," I hear him tell my mother.

"Hello," my mother says her voice still thick with sleep. Unlike me and my father, she does not find it the least bit shameful to still be in bed sleeping at 7:30 A.M.

"I can't get my big girl panties on this morning," I say into my phone. "I'm stuck, I don't want to drive over and feed the dog today."

"Then don't, honey," my mother's sleepy voice answers back. "We can stop tomorrow on our way to breakfast. I don't think missing one day will hurt."

"Ugh," I groan into the phone. "Do you know the value of a good intention if you're backing it up with empty fucking bullshit? Nothing, Mom, it's worth absolutely nothing." My frustrated, profane and nonsensical question that wasn't really a question has my mother chuckling.

"I'm not sure what that means, honey" is all she says.

"I'm pulling out," I tell her, "just stay on the phone with me until I get there."

I can sense her repositioning herself in bed to stay on the phone with me.

"What's on our agenda for tomorrow?" she asks me.

There it is; no judgment, no advice, no opinion, just presence. How does one learn that?

"I'm pulling in. I think I'm good now, Mom. Thanks. If I'm not at the house in the morning when you come to pick me up, you know where to look for my body," I say laughing.

"I don't always think you're funny." My mother says in a scolding tone, "but you're doing a good thing."

"Thanks, Mom. See you tomorrow," and I hang up.

I hop out of my truck and cross the road. If anyone is watching me, I'm sure that everything would look perfectly normal for a woman walking into the woods with a plastic grocery bag, but I am still in a heightened state. I am not having a panic attack, but I definitely do not feel grounded either. As I walk through the woods to the barn, I fight the urge to run, dump the food and water into the bowls, and run back out. However, I have learned that there is no such thing as out-maneuvering anxiety. The more frantic I become in my attempts to evade it, the more momentum it gains. I am acutely aware of the location of my phone and absently tap my pocket several times to confirm its existence. "Stay here, stay here," I coach myself, "in this moment, with this purpose." And I force a deep breath. My anxiety provokes a compulsion to flee. It has two components to it. The first is a hyper sensitivity to my physical body, and the second is an emotional denial of the moment. I stop walking about twenty feet away from the barn. "I am a screen," I say out loud, my eyes closed and my arms raised slightly away from my sides.

This self-prompting instantly creates a visual for me that provides an immediate measure of relief. I see myself as a giant, human-shaped window screen, with thousands of little holes that allow fear and anxiousness to pass through me. I am learning to consciously accept the "noise" of fear into my space. Over the years I have discovered that emotionally 'hugging' my fear is a lot less terrifying than wrestling with it. Like a naughty, undisciplined child, it wants to be heard and acknowledged. My desperate past attempts to stop the momentum of my anxiety remind me of my once painful school-girl struggle to keep a fair-weather friend from making a privately divulged secret into a public proclamation in the middle of the junior high cafeteria: humiliating, terrifying and ultimately futile. It's been liberating to learn that I can actually sit with my discomfort and realize I will not die from it. Imperfection, emotionally honesty, and vulnerability are my truth, as is my willingness to love and accept myself. Who knew I had been standing in the light of the Universe all along? ....I've simply had my eyes squeezed shut!

Once I have filled both bowls, I head back out of the barn. I feel relief. I pause at the threshold and recite the Prayer of Protection on behalf of the dog. At the end of the prayer, I ask the Angels and Fairies to have a chat with my friend that dwells in the barn, to let her know that if she can trust me, I want to help her. As I walk through the woods, I stick my arms out in front of my body like Frankenstein and take a few straight-legged steps bellowing in my best monster voice, "I am alive! I am alive!"

I laugh at myself, but my silly affirmation leaves me feeling more confident and content than I was heading in. Back in my truck, I click on my phone to assure myself that it is working and head home to the farm.

I'll Come up With My Own Labels, Thank You!

"How's the friendly neighborhood dog rescuer?" Craig asks one morning.

"Funny thing about that," I say to him, my head cocked off to the side, "I hate that word. It sounds arrogant. I'll be the friendly neighborhood dog advocate."

I steer clear of perceiving myself as a rescuer. That can be an emotional Pandora's Box. One of the human ego's favorite feasts is a giant platter of, "aren't I wonderful!" with complimentary side dishes of rationalization and false humility. I know that this cannot be about me. If I take on the "rescuer" persona, I risk everything - - my integrity with the Universe and her safety in the woods, for starters.

I honestly can't remember the last time someone has mentioned their dog to me that they haven't labeled it a "rescue." Nowadays, it seems as though a pet needs to be more than a great companion in its own right. It also needs to exist as a symbol of its human's good character. You never hear anyone say, "I contacted a reputable breeder, picked out a puppy, paid a ridiculous sum of money, and, ta-da, we have a new family pet!

I have kept my mission quiet with the exception of a few close and trustworthy people. I am insistent with my mom that she not discuss this situation with her circle of friends and explain to her that if we really want to protect the dog, it has to remain something of a secret until I can get her out of the woods. There would be no malice intended on their part, but their "discretion filter," as I call it, with regard to their families' personal lives, apparently shuts off when they sit down to sew or play cards together.

I appreciate passionate people and consider myself one of them. But, I have watched the drama of a desperate animal unfold, and suddenly every dog lover, do-gooder, self-proclaimed animal expert, attention seeker and nut job are invading the animal's space, often resulting in the unfortunate and unnecessary end to an animal they all professed to be trying to save. I think oftentimes what initially has the appearance of a good deed involving animals or people turns at some point into a need for individual recognition. The draw to the spotlight becomes paramount over the survival and subsequent life quality of the sufferer they profess to be helping. Once the spotlight fades, or immediate resolution with a round of applause and accolades doesn't manifest, good intentions often seem to fade too. So what is my motive in this situation? Karma is my simplest answer. To share with her what so many have shared with me: understanding, affection and hope.

The following morning, my mother pulls in and honks the horn, as usual, just in case I didn't hear the five dogs running through the house, blasting out the dog door and barking at the fence. I am always annoyed.

"Honestly you guys, shut up!" I yell toward the occupants of the back yard as I climb into the passenger seat of my mom's beige Nissan, plastic bag in hand.

"Jesus crimeany," I lament, settling into the seat and pulling my seat belt across my lap.

"Good morning, sunshine." My mom is grinning like a Cheshire cat and pats me on the thigh.

"Just for the record," I say drolly, "I don't always think you're funny either" and my mom chuckles.

"I see we're off to visit the dog," my mom says glancing at the bag in my lap before putting the car in reverse.

"I'm off to visit the dog," I respond, "it will take less than ten minutes total,"

"I'd like to walk back with you and see where she lives," my mom says, sounding a little hurt.

"I know you would, mom, and I'd like you to see it too, but I think bringing another scent into the woods will make her even more leery than she already is. I'm trying to make her feel cared for, not pursued. I don't want her to get nervous and take off."

"Oh, I wouldn't want her to take off either," my mom says, with both sincerity and concern.

"Right there," I say pointing, and my mom pulls into the driveway belonging to empathetic neighbor.

"Two shakes," I say hopping out and closing the door. I glance in both directions and jog across the road.

Today I am wearing a "going to town" pair of shoes, not the heavier farm boots I usually wear on this outing. My trek through the leaves is noticeably quieter, and I take quick, fast steps, almost like a jog until I am just thirty feet or so from the entrance of the barn. I stop dead in my tracks as I catch sight of her. It is just her backside I see, brown coloring and a docked tail, I think, as she walks purposefully into the hedgerow. She makes a left turn, goes to the backside of the chicken coop and turns back around so she is standing facing me. It's no wonder I haven't been able to see her. It's like she's dressed in camo, blending in perfectly with her drab, late autumn surroundings. It is mostly just her eyes that are visible, but only because I know where to look.

"Hey, sweet pea," I coo to her, squatting down and resting my forearms on my knees in a relaxed pose. "Want to go for a ride in Grandma's car?" I ask her.

But she is unimpressed with my offer and stands silently staring at me. "Ok for you," I tell her.

I walk into the barn and re-fill the bowls on the floor, turn around and walk back out. I stand just outside the door and look back to where she was standing. For a moment I think that she has moved, but then I catch sight of her eyes again. She is still holding her intent gaze.

"Last chance today, love bug," I call to her. "No one brings me my breakfast, and my momma's buying today, so I'm outta here."

I pause, "Come on, girl," I say in a pleading tone. "If you walk out of here with me right now, I'll buy you eggs and bacon." She holds statue-still and continues to stare.

"See ya tomorrow, girl." I say and walk back towards the road.

"Holy crap, Mom!" I say as I climb back into my mother's car. "I actually saw her."

"Oh, you're kidding," my mom replies, sounding just as delighted as I am.

"Did you get close to her?" she asks, "Can you tell what kind of dog it is? Is it a Pit Bull like you thought it might be?" My mom's string of questions is delaying our departure, and I am starving.

"No, to all of the above." is my brief answer. "Let's head to breakfast, and I'll tell you on the way."

"So how many more days do you plan to feed her, honey?" my mom asks me when the waitress is done taking our order.

I rummage around in my purse for a minute and reply with mock dismay, "I have once again left the house without my crystal ball, so I am unable to answer the question."

"You're such a smart ass," my mom says with a wry smile.

I place my right forearm and left elbow on the table and drop my chin into my left hand, sigh, and look at my mom. My demeanor is softer and more serious now.

"How could I stop feeding her now?" It is not just a question directed solely to my mother, it is *the* question. But discussing it out loud with my mom has suddenly made the answer clear to me.

"I will stop feeding her when she either leaves the woods with me or she isn't there to feed anymore," I say. "I won't just vaporize and not be there for her, just like you've never not been there for me." I smile over at my mom, and we both have tears in our eyes.

Stubbornness in Its Sunday Best..... I'll call it Fortitude

Feeding the dog in the woods has become a built-in part of my day. Most mornings I go alone, but on a few occasions when I have felt a little anxious, I have taken Buddy, Rose or Kaya to accompany me in the truck. Picking up a load of hay every week is also part of my routine, so I keep in regular contact with Curlers regarding the dog.

"Oh yeah, she's definitely warming up to me." I tell her. "I should have my hands on her in a few days," which is complete crap, but I don't want her son to trump my efforts with a shotgun.

The mornings are definitely getting colder as the weeks have passed. Today, I am donning a bright orange knitted hat I purchased at the farm store yesterday. It is deer hunting season, and I definitely want to be visible to anyone close enough to see me or hear me walking through the woods.

I am cranky this morning. "It's just me," I announce, hiking up to the entrance of the old barn. I stop just outside of the doorway and turn around, facing the general direction of the tree line where she hides when I'm here.

"I have this God-awful hat on, covering an extremely unflattering hairdo," I yell out, "because if I get shot, your

114

morning room service at this crappy, one star accommodation is gonna' come to a screeching halt." I sound exasperated.

"Suit yourself," are my parting words.

As I stomp away from the barn, I feel the weight of sadness. I never imagined that this would go on for so long. I am worried about the increasingly colder temperatures, especially at night. I am worried about the emotional toll of her dreary isolation, and I am disheartened at her complete distrust of any interaction with me. I briefly contemplate bringing over a warm dog bed, but veto the idea, reminding myself I do not want this to be her permanent home or my permanent assignment.

I feel like something needs to change. We have both become too comfortable with this routine, and I am no closer to my goal of getting her out of this situation. If I get more people involved, I risk her running away and getting so spooked she won't come back to the barn, and then, what are the odds of her finding another isolated, safe shelter in the Michigan winter and someone to feed her? Absolutely zero. Or worse yet, making her feel trapped and confronted, provoking a behavior that is possibly misinterpreted as aggression. I'm not sure how I would handle that. Nope, she and I will have to figure this out. So, I decide instead to increase her food ration because trying to stay warm burns calories.

Back in Black

We arrive at the funeral home for the first session of visitation. My sister, surrogate sister, and I are dressed in our newly purchased black outfits. We had joked on the way to the mall that we were dedicating our shopping trip to our mom. Every family member is present, including the departed Matriarch, whose body is already staged in the main viewing room. When I reach the threshold, the scene in front of me is so deeply heartbreaking, I am momentarily paralyzed. Standing alone at the casket is my daughter. She is approximately two weeks away from the birth of her first child, a daughter. I have been concerned that the stress of my mother's death would be the final straw in an already horrendous pregnancy experience that would send her into labor. Her left hand is resting on her enormous belly, and her right hand is resting tentatively on my mother's cold hands. My daughter has suffered through eight and a half months of the most dreadful pregnancy I have ever witnessed, hospitalized at least five times with severe bouts of nausea, vomiting and dehydration. My mother was her rock through the entire process, helping her wash all the baby clothes received at her showers, putting together furniture, painting the nursery and organizing all things "baby" in their newly-purchased home. At that moment, I am more devastated for my daughter than I am for anyone else, myself included.

This main part of the funeral home, like the "showroom of death" is fashioned in the same décor; mentally I have dubbed it, "deceased chic." Yesterday, my sister and I picked out of our mother's closet a favorite Wedgewood-china-blue dress that was delivered to the funeral home to be arranged on her body for the open casket viewing, another decision we had all agreed upon. Accompanying my mother's body, draped across the closed, bottom half of the casket is a beautiful quilt that she had recently completed titled, "spring." The quilt is stunning, its fabrics consist of rich, muted shades of blues and greens and purples. The casket is surrounded by an overwhelming array of cut flower arrangements, plants and statuary that have been sent by friends and acquaintances. The fragrant blooms and greenery are almost floor to ceiling on both sides of the casket. Coupled with the blue dress and the stunning quilt, it is a tragically lovely ensemble.

The early visitation is packed. People are at the door waiting to enter and come up the stairs where our father and the three of us "kids" are in a receiving line greeting people and accepting condolences. The rest of the family is milling around close by. It seems as though the majority of people in attendance knew my mother through her vast and varied activities in the community. Even though I live locally, many of these people are strangers to me. Conversations with visitors run the gambit, from awkward to deeply moving. I am momentarily embarrassed following a missed cue between a handshake and a hug, and then just as quickly moved to tears as a young woman shares her story about how important and influential my mother was to her as her high school tennis coach and teenage sounding board.

Toward the end of this first viewing, when there is brief respite from the flow of people, a "married in" family member is compelled to bring to my attention that I have sounded like a broken record for the past two hours; "Hi I'm Laura, and I'm the youngest. Hi, I'm Laura, I'm the youngest" she mimics. I am aware that a few family members within earshot are pausing, waiting to see how I will respond, but I am already too deflated and now self-conscious to formulate a retort. Her sardonic little jab, delivered with her signature chuckle, has hit its intended mark. I just shrug my shoulders, not surprised that even this somber occasion cannot curb her natural inclination toward condescension and criticism. Shortly after, when my husband and I climb into our car following the first visitation, and the vehicle she is riding in drives past us on its way out of the parking lot, I vigorously flip her off - - down below the window line of course, we have enough family drama right now. A steady stream of frustrated, nonsensical profanity spews out of my mouth. Once they are past us and out of view, I am gesturing wildly, above the window line now, "Are you fucking kidding me? You self-entitled bitch!" My animated display has my husband, and eventually me, laughing for the first time in days.

Two hours later when the evening visitation begins, a late winter storm has blown in and given rise to a veritable blizzard outside. People entering the funeral home are stomping their feet, brushing snow off their coats and commenting on the treacherous road conditions. It is humbling to see all the people who have ventured out in this weather to pay their respects to my mother and offer condolences to my family. Their kindness is a soothing salve on our open wound.

"Dad!" My husband and I both turn, when we hear an anguished plea coming from our daughter a few feet away. My husband immediately breaks away from our conversation turns to our daughter standing next to her cousin. Both girls are visibly distraught. "Jesus, dad, get him away from there before I kill him" she is pleading and pointing toward the casket. My husband is already striding up to our eleven-year-old nephew who is standing, hands on his hips, beaming. He has spent the last hour or so acting as if his grandmother's dead body is a carnival attraction. He is animated, giddy and obsessively wiping his sweaty palms on the front of his now rumpled dress pants and then pretending to smooth and straighten the quilt on the casket. He makes a point of introducing himself to every person who walks towards my mother's body and is accompanying people, chatting non-stop, as they walk up to pay their respects. He is undaunted, even by the mourners who do not acknowledge him. When my husband approaches him, scowling and giving him the "come here" index finger signal, the boy audibly sighs, hangs his head and looks instantly deflated. As the two walk past me, my husband's hand firmly on our nephew's shoulder, the boy looks up at me and shrugs as if to say "Oh well, it was fun while it lasted." "We're gonna go take a break in the kid's play room," my husband says in a low voice.

Deep exhaustion has everyone in the family appearing more relaxed as the evening comes to a close. Many of my close friends are in attendance. They have braved the hazardous driving conditions, paid their respects and extended condolences to my father and siblings and are now standing together, chatting and laughing quietly, in no apparent hurry to leave. For the first time since my mother's passing, as I merge into this gathering and receive a group hug, I feel a sense of belonging that helps ground and comfort me. I am surprised at how important it is that they are here with me. These people are part of my pack.

Allowing

Come, come, whoever you are, wanderer, worshiper,
lover of leaving. It doesn't matter. Ours is not a caravan
of despair. Come, even if you have broken your vows
a thousand times. Come, yet again, come, come.

~ Rumi

Rose 2012

I know four truths about my parents:

1.) They have always loved each other.
2.) They cherish their family above all else.
3.) They are die-hard animal lovers.
4.) They are abundantly generous.

My earliest memory of my parents' devotion to a family pet was when we moved across the country from California to Pennsylvania in the early 1970's. Our family turtle, Tommy, whom I had purchased at Woolworths with my accrued allowance, was carried aboard the plane by my father in a white Chinese food take-out box. During the flight, every half hour or so, my father would leave his seat and enter the airplanes tiny bathroom holding the little white box, fill the sink with water and let Tommy have a brief swim to keep his shell moist. My mother had packed everyone snacks for the flight, including Tommy. We all arrived safe and sound on the East Coast, where Tommy lived for several more years. When he finally met his end, my mother carefully placed him inside an empty jewelry box atop the white cotton square and taped it closed. My father led a heartfelt funeral service that several of the neighborhood kids attended and ceremoniously buried him under one of the pine trees in our front yard.

My family's history could be marked by the succession of pets, each one a much loved and valuable member of the family. Even though my siblings and I departed our parents' house decades ago, there continues to be an assortment of four-legged residents that call it home.

Based on my childhood history with animals, it is not surprising that today I am tethered to this wise and gentle soul named Rose, a female Great Pyrenees of unknown age. Like the strong female energies before her, she has been sent, no doubt, to help me find my way. My mother's unforeseen death plummeted me into a desperately sad place, but, as I begin the arduous journey of slowly but steadily emerging from the dense, oppressive fog of grief, sitting in front of me, patiently waiting in the misty dawn of my future, is Rose. Like that of her predecessors, Roses' presence and influence serves as much needed air in the sometimes flat tire moments of my life. "I wonder if I'm the only human that has to take their Guardian Angel to the groomer." I often tease her.

Rose is no ordinary dog. She is always composed. Even in moments of play, her artless grace is both admirable and enviable. Rose has weathered her own storm as a malnourished and abandoned stray on her journey into my life where she stands now as both my steadfast companion and undisputed Matriarch of my dog pack. Like everything else we draw into our lives, her timing was impeccable. Five uneventful months after her arrival home with me in September of 2009 from a horse show at the Kentucky horse park in Lexington, my mother is gone.

Gratitude

It is Rose's statesmanlike composure during the aftermath of my mother's death that has me looking at her, and life, in a new light. For the first time in my all my years surrounded by animals, it is a true epiphany to realize I am in no way a superior species, just different. My shocking awareness that life really is as fleeting as my grandmother warned me it was, coupled with a somewhat desperate need to feel both alive and a contributor, I begin to comb the internet in search of therapy dog certification programs. My mother had remarked many times that volunteering, "gave her a better perspective on life," and, I am in desperate need of a better perspective. What I do not know at the onset of this new chapter, is how deeply I will be affected and permanently changed by my journey with Rose. She will be both my chaperone and mentor me as we move forward together. Rose reveals to me, a level of understanding and appreciation that will expand my human experience in ways I could never have imagined.

My best kept secret is that I am not a gifted dog handler. I have a gifted dog. Rose passes the certification test, methodically moving through each element required, with me feeling like an imposter at the end of the leash. My saving grace are her eyes. Each time my trembling hand reaches down to stroke her body for reassurance, she gazes up at me with the steady and tolerant expression of a parent. "This is our dharma," she tells me, "we will do this together." And, so we do. For two years now, since the late spring of 2010, I have been the benefactor of Rose's popularity and intuition. What I enjoy most about our time spent volunteering at the local hospital is people's genuine delight and gratitude for Roses' presence.

I'm Sonny to Her Cher

"Oh my God, is this a therapy dog?" My girl Rose is, at the moment, the focal point in the hospital lobby thanks to the woman who is speed-walking toward us, squealing.

"Yes, she is a therapy dog," I chuckle. I barely have the chance to finish, and she is talking again.

"Oh you have to go see my dad! Can you go see my dad? She *has* to go see my dad!"

"We'd love to go see your dad, wouldn't we, Rose?" I look down for confirmation from my fluffy, white companion, and she doesn't let me down. Rose looks directly at my face, as if to calmly say, "Certainly, let's go see the dad."

"What's his room number?" I ask, removing a pen and rumpled piece of used scratch paper from the pocket of my green, hospital-issue volunteer smock. I scribble down the number she recites and circle it several times so I remember which of the many numbers on the paper I'm heading to this evening. In that moment, I once again promise myself that I will get a fresh piece of scratch paper.

"Oh, he's gonna love this," she says looking at her watch. "I have to step out, but thank you, and thank you, big doggie!" she says bending forward and ruffling the long, thick fur on Rose's neck. Because she approached us as she came off the elevator headed toward the main door I am assuming that she is on her way home for the evening.

Rose and I ride the elevator and step off at the seventh floor. As we round the corner, headed towards the nurse's station at the start of the hallway, Rose is immediately spotted. One of the nurses on duty this evening always says the same thing when she spots Rose walking down the hallway, "Here comes my favorite dog in the whole world!" I have actually never asked her, but I am assuming she either doesn't have a dog, or if she does, it's a naughty one.

If any of the hospital staff acknowledges me, which they often do not, it is always secondary to their engaging with Rose. It reminds me of something I said to my husband one time when he mentioned that I treated my clients and students better than I treated him: "Sometimes I use all my happy up on the people that pay for it," I told him. I often get that same feeling from nurses. I imagine they only have so much of themselves to emotionally pour into a twelve-hour shift, and their patients, rightfully so, are the main recipients of their "happy." Rose is a contributor here, not a taker. Her presence runs the full gambit: everything from a momentary distraction to comforter and confidante. She is the undisputed star of our traveling show. I am very comfortable as an "extra" on the set.

A few of the nurses and other staff members have gathered just outside the nurses' station to visit with Rose. While they are cooing and fussing over her, my mind drifts back to a memorable visit that took place last winter, almost at the very spot where we are standing now. It is the evening of Christmas day. Rose and I round the corner of this hallway and encounter a large group of visitors, the overflow of an already, jam-packed patient room. Based on the scene, I make the assumption they are all related. Their conversations have the easy chatter of familiarity, and every one of them is dressed in their holiday finest including the children. My guess is that the patient is a family elder. The adults are enjoying their banter back and forth. I catch snippets of a cooking conversation from the women, and a few of the men are having an animated, friendly debate about the anticipated New Year's Day football outcomes. One bored, resentful-looking teenager is leaning against the wall, arms folded and staring at the floor. His long bangs are covering his face, and every thirty seconds or so he shakes his head to the side in a goofy, awkward teenage gesture meant to adjust his hair without changing his "I hate that I'm here" pose. A group of younger children, both boys and girls, entertain themselves with the customary "cousins gathering" standards of pushing, pulling, slapping and running. I hear someone yell, "Kids!" at least three times since stepping off the elevator.

I can see the adults immediate relief when Rose and I approach, providing a distraction for the children, a distraction that comes complete with adult supervision…. me. The collection of youngsters is thrilled at the unexpected sight of a giant white dog inside the hospital and quickly descends on her. They assemble themselves all the way around her body, some standing, some dropping to their knees on the floor, every one of them reaching out to touch her back and head, running their fingers over and through her thick fur. An adorable little toddler, perhaps two or three years old, plops himself directly in front of her and begins asking Rose questions, which I take the liberty of answering for her. As is the norm with visitors of all ages,

Rose's presence immediately prompts them to share stories about their own pets.

Everyone is delighted. Everyone, that is, except a lovely little girl with a head full of cascading auburn ringlets, dressed in a sparkly holiday dress complete with sparkly tights and shiny, black dress flats with satin bows on the toes. She is standing apart from the other children. I am guessing she's around eight or nine. "What's the matter, honey, don't you like dogs?" I ask her.

For a moment she just stares blankly at me. "She's hairy," she responds, admonishingly, stating the obvious, but somehow making it sound villainous.

"Ahhh," I nod my head up and down, "That's true, she is very hairy," I say. "I think all girls wished they had thick, beautiful hair like you and Rose, don't you?"

This seemingly self-assured little darling has her arms folded tightly across her chest, chin down and is making direct, unwavering eye contact with me. I am kneeling next to the group of kids and Rose who has succumbed to our stationary position and laid down.

"She's a dog." She practically spits the words out at me, and for a split second I expect to hear her add, "Dumbass!" but she simply continues to glare. She reminds me of a female Chihuahua that joined my pack after displaying behaviors that deemed her unadoptable at the county dog pound: growling, teeth barring and antisocial.

"Shut up, Elizabeth," one of the older boys says, "you're *such a brat*!" He makes his statement emphatically, momentarily glaring back at her. I can see the familial resemblance. This must be big brother.

"You shut up," she throws back the classic sibling response while simultaneously striking a pose: one foot forward, something similar to fourth position in ballet, one hand on her hip and returning her brother's stare with a steely expression complete with pursed mouth and knitted brow. Her demeanor is in complete contrast with her charming holiday attire. I can't help but think that Elizabeth's mother must be a peach. I watch in awe as she makes her next move. Without taking her eyes off the group of youngsters gathered around Rose, (my Chihuahua does this too!) she strides toward me and plucks the leash out of my hand. "Why do **you** have to be with her?" the venom laden question makes its unlikely exit from the tiny, rose-lipped mouth. There is an audible gasp from Rose's fan club. I feel like I'm on the playground, and Elizabeth just threw the first punch. She is flipping the handle of the leash back and forth in front of her body, daring me to re-claim it. Rose has lowered her head to the floor. She is content to rest on the cool tile, completely unconcerned that this pint-sized Medusa is currently in control of her leash.

I don't reach for the leash. I don't even flinch. This child is clearly hoping…..praying for an opening that will facilitate her attention-seeking behavior. I shuffle through my emotional Rolodex looking for an appropriate response. If she were part of my pack, canine or human, my response would likely be swift and deliberate. There would be no doubt that I viewed this behavior as a breech in the code of appropriate conduct. But fortunately she is not part of my pack.

"You're such a beautiful girl, Elizabeth, doesn't it feel yucky to act so ugly?" I pose my question slowly and deliberately, never breaking eye contact with her, but keeping my expression relaxed and detached. I immediately sense that my hunch is correct, Elizabeth is used to a steady diet of empty threats and high drama. I have caught her off guard. She is no longer flipping the handle of the leash from side to side. I extend my open palm and hold it out in front of her. Her gaze wavers at my gesture, and I am watching her deflate. The leash is as good as mine; I just have to wait for her to process this non-verbal exchange. I have known many "Elizabeth's." They are much more comfortable reacting to a situation. Already at this young and tender age she is mastering the nuances of the passive-aggressive female: waiting…hoping to be offended so she can validate her existence and justify her actions through the condemnation and blaming of others. I have dubbed her generation, "The Finger Pointers," and it looks like she'll be a leader. I'm sure if you ask my own child, my errors as a parent have been numerous, but I am proud of the fact that my daughter was raised to be respectful of the feelings of others and to own her attitudes and decisions. However, if I could go back in time, I would spend less time telling my child how to be a good girl and a lot more time talking about what "good" feels like on the inside.

The proverbial wind has left Elizabeth's sails, and for a moment I get a glimpse of the little girl behind the giant attitude. She unceremoniously drops the leash into my open hand. As she turns to walk away, I pipe up, "Hey, don't you want to know why I have to be with Rose?" To my delight, she turns back and faces me, "Why?" she asks, a flicker of interest flashing in her eyes. "I have to be with Rose because I can do two things she can't do: I have to drive the car and push the elevator buttons." One again I watch as Elizabeth processes what I have told her.

"You could teach her to push the buttons, you know," and she turns around and flounces back toward the gathering of adults.

Someone has asked me a question, "I'm sorry, I zoned out for a minute," I say, refocusing on the dog and people in front of me, "What was that?"

"How old is Rose?" one of the nurses asks.

"She's a senior according to the condition of her teeth. I adopted her in Kentucky in 2008, and she was a full-fledged adult dog then, so I am guessing she's somewhere between eight and ten," I tell her. While Rose is being fussed over I hear an unusually loud, tense-sounding discussion coming from one of the patient rooms behind me. I hear a door open and close, and then a familiar voice says, "Oh you're here!" and, as I turn around, I am surprised to see the woman from the lobby.

While my head is still turned, one of the nurses asks me quietly, "Is that a room request?"

I turn back and make eye contact with the nurse, answering the question with a slight nod yes, and ask my own silent question with raised brows. The nurse gives a small nod and silently mouths the word "No." Another nod toward the door, and I follow her eyes to a sign stating that visitors are prohibited in that patient room. What a bummer! she was so excited about the prospect of a visit.

"I'm afraid Rose won't be able to go in and see your dad today. I'm so sorry," I tell her, "we aren't allowed to enter a patient room that has visitor restrictions." As my statement sinks in, she sighs, and the look of disappointment on the woman's face makes my heart hurt.

"I'm so sorry," I say again. "They just don't want one of us to unknowingly bring something harmful into your dad's room."

"I know" she says, her voice thick with sadness and resignation. "It just seems stupid at this point." Tears are welling up, and she swipes her hand impatiently across her face, "It's not like it's going to change anything, and I know he would love to see her."

I pull my travel pack off my shoulder, unzip it and fish out one of Rose's custom calling cards. "You can show him a picture, and let him know that Rose stopped to say hello," I say, trying to sound upbeat. On the front of the card is a black and white copy of an artist's rendering of Rose, originally done in pen and ink. Across the bottom is an inscription that reads: "Cold nose and warm wishes, Rose" On the backside of the card is a small bio along with some interesting facts about the Great Pyrenees breed. I hand her the card, and she stares at it, unsure of what to do with it. Receiving a post card was not how she envisioned this encounter. She leans her shoulder against the wall and slowly slides her weight down until she is squatting next to Rose.

"Thank you anyway, Rose. I appreciate you coming up here. At least….. I got to meet you." Her voice is thick and strained.

I notice that Rose's attention shifts slightly, and she is staring at the closed door of the patient room. I am not surprised when momentarily it opens. An older woman walks out and slowly closes the door behind her.

"Awe, this must be the therapy dog from the lobby my daughter was telling us about." she says as she turns around to face us.

There is no answer from the woman squatting down, so I respond, "Yes, this is Rose. I was just explaining to your daughter that I won't be able to do a room visit because of the visitor restrictions," and again, the younger woman snorts her disapproval of the situation.

"I'm sorry," I say again to fill in the gap of silence.

I look back to the two sitting on the floor. The daughter is on her knees facing Rose. Silent tears are streaming down her face as she rubs Rose's chin. Rose is engaging two of the super powers of her one-dog ministry: companionable silence and patience. I look back at the mother apologetically. She takes a step toward her daughter and lightly places her hand upon the younger woman's back.

"Don't, Mom," the daughter shrugs her body away from her mother's offending hand. She sits down on the floor, back against the wall and looks inconsolable. Rose's attention stays with the daughter but mine shifts for a moment, and I notice that the staff have all gone back to their duties. One of the nurses is now staring at computer screens a few feet away from where I am standing. That is another element of time inside a hospital, the dynamics can shift quickly.

"Do you mind if I pet the dog?" the mother asks tentatively.

The question brings my attention back, and I start to answer but realize that the mother has directed the question to the daughter, not to me.

"I don't care if you pet the dog or not, Mom," the daughter sighs and closes her eyes, resting her head back against the wall.

"Coming down," the mother announces. Her right arm is outstretched, palm against the wall to steady herself. The daughter's eyes are open now, and I watch both of them as the mother slowly lowers her body until she too is sitting on the floor, legs outstretched, next to her daughter. The tears have begun again.

As if she had been waiting patiently for her guests to be seated first, Rose takes her turn and lowers herself down. She is lying with her chest and legs across the daughter's lap, her front paws resting against the mother's thigh.

The daughter attempts to laugh at Rose's gesture, but it comes out as a choked sob, "I just want things to go back to normal, Mom," she says, resting her head against her mother's shoulder.

"We all do, honey," the mom says, tears now streaming down her face. She reaches her left arm across her body and cups her daughter's face in her hand, "We all do," the mother says again with a tired sigh.

As I gaze at the scene, I am struck by a moment of deep envy. *I* want things to be back to normal too, my heart cries. Why couldn't this be my mother and I consoling each other on the hospital floor?

I let the leather leash slide off my wrist and quietly set it down. I walk to the nurse's station in an attempt to allow this moment the privacy it deserves. I notice one of the nurses dabbing tears from her face.

Rose is the conduit here. She is the connection that creates a neutral space for these two sad hearts to sit together in their suffering. I can see and feel the energetic shift as these woman find strength in their love for each other and in their shared love of the man who lies dying in the hospital room behind the closed door. I am acutely aware that he is not the one the Universe sent Rose here to heal.

I do not want to be an intruder, but I am close enough to keep an eye on my girl, and to overhear snippets of conversation about pets and kids and reminiscence of family. When I turn back around a few minutes later, they are both laughing, and Rose has raised herself back up on her feet and is stretching. "I think she's done with these two crying woman," the mother says. I walk over and pick up the leash, and Rose looks up at me.

"Actually", I say "I think she knows she isn't needed anymore." And I smile at the two women still sitting on the floor.

"I can't tell you what this has meant to us," the daughter says, holding her mother's hand. "Sitting here together, petting Rose and talking about our dogs, our kids and our lives outside the hospital, life before this horrible illness...... it has been like having a piece of home and comfort with us tonight. We're so grateful."

"Thank you so much", the mother chimes in, wiping her eyes, "This is a beautiful gesture, sharing your dog with us."

"You're very welcome," I smile, "and for my part, how about I help you two get up off the floor?" and we all laugh as I reach down to give them my hand.

Both women say a final "thank you" to Rose, and I get a hug from both the mother and daughter. For a moment

I want to tell them to hold on tight to each other, but this is their story, so I wave goodnight as Rose and I walk away.

When we enter the quiet of the elevator, my mind recalls a sarcastic question from a curmudgeon seated in the hospital lobby, "So, your dog just walks around the hospital?" He sounded almost disgusted. "Yes sir," I replied politely, "she just walks around the hospital."

A New Patient

"Holy cow, what happened to this guy?" asks Dr. Margaret as I carry in my large, yellow bundle of tragedy.

"I'm assuming the first strike was getting separated from his people, and I have no idea how that happened," I say over my shoulder as I lay him, left side down, on the floor of her tiny exam room. "His second strike was an obvious close encounter with a vehicle, and his third strike was to end up laying in the dog pound for ten days slowly dying of despair."

"Hmmmm," says Dr. Margaret, "I hate to add insult to injury, as they say, but let's start by taking your temperature, boy." She runs her hand down the exposed right side of his body. When she reaches the sagging depression where a hip should be, she shakes her head and tells him, "That can't feel great, buddy," and continues down to lift his tail and slide the lubricated thermometer in his butt. When the thermometer beeps, indicating it's finished, she extracts it, glances at the digital read-out and replaces it in the pocket of her scrubs. I am resting my butt on the edge of a chair in the corner of the exam room. The yellow dog is at my feet, and I am leaning over him, lightly stroking his head. I have petted a lot of dogs in my day, but never one as soft as this. It feels like he has rabbit fur. I cannot help but consider the contrast between his depressing circumstances and his warm, sunny yellow coloring.

Dr. Margaret has been kneeling on the floor next to him. She scoots herself a foot or two toward his head and pulls back his top lip to examine his teeth and gums. "Geez, this dog isn't very old," she says, "I'd say just a year or two, three at the most. He's got all adult teeth, but they're bright white, no tartar line." She grabs the edge of the exam table and struggles a moment or two to shift her weight off her knees and onto her feet. When she finally stands, she continues to hold the edge of the table and takes a few heaving, asthmatic breaths to catch her wind.

Dr. Margaret is one of my favorite people currently on the planet. I met her many years ago through our mutual connection to horses. We spent years as seasonal friends, enjoying each other's company and catching up on life several times during the spring and summer while attending the same horse shows. Two years before, she became a client at my farm, and our friendship has blossomed. Despite the fact that I have a wonderful relationship with our local vet who has always worked on our large and small animals, I have begun to call on Margaret more and more often for our dogs. She and I pull off a very successful juggling act of veterinarian and client, instructor and student, all built on a solid foundation of mutual admiration.

From the onset, Margaret has always seemed to me very extraordinary. I have watched with interest over the years as people respond to her bi-polar eccentricities that often illustrate the intense extremes between mania and depression. I am drawn to her quirkiness, and even though she is ten years my senior, I am compelled toward a big sister protectiveness. She is a veritable casserole, a host of seemingly incompatible physical and emotional ingredients thrown together with an outcome that is both surprising and wonderful. In addition to being bipolar, Margaret has ADHD, mild dyslexia, severe asthma, and debilitating migraine headaches. She has struggled with alcohol and prescription drug addiction and is a breast cancer survivor; all of this is topped off, literally, with a genius IQ.

Dr. Margaret is an articulate, compassionate and deeply intuitive practitioner. I think when she is practicing medicine, the world makes the most sense to her. Even in a situation like this, with an animal that is in dire straits, her demeanor is calm and confident.

My experiences with her as "Dr. Margaret," inside the scope of our veterinarian-to-client relationship, are often in direct contrast to the Margaret who is herself the client and student. That Margaret is prone to dramatic, emotional displays. She is often ravaged by insecurity and fear. Her expressions of her own success or failure with regard to her athletic abilities as a rider are often indistinguishable: whether disappointed or euphoric, she will sit on top of her horse hyperventilating, sobbing and communicating through a largely undecipherable dialogue. Bystanders of every age watch fascinated at the outpouring of raw, unfiltered emotion. In my mind and heart, I see Margaret as a spiritual turtle somehow hatching and surviving into this lifetime without the benefit of the protective shell that most of us are wearing to bolster her physically and buffer her emotionally from the human experience. She steadfastly crawls through life, persevering despite the struggles. She is a beautiful soul and definitely one of my heroes.

"Well, I'm not sure what's going on there," she says, pointing to his hindquarter, "but the most immediate problem is how dehydrated he is, and obviously he's in a great deal of pain. I'm gonna hook him up to IV fluids and give him some of "the good stuff," for pain that will probably keep him pretty sleepy. We'll take a good look at him either tomorrow or Monday, when I have some help to get X-rays, Ok?" she says, looking directly at me. "You know he's fine here, Laura. I'll be in and out constantly to check on him, and I'll stay in touch. You know that."

"I know that," I nod.

"Let's help him up, and we'll go make him comfy in a kennel." Margaret takes hold of the leash that's been lying on the floor. I lean over him, one foot on each side of his body, and wrap my arms around his ribcage, hands under his belly, and lift him off the floor. Once standing, I swing my leg over, bend down and cradle his body, right arm around the front of his chest and left arm under his butt. "Here we go," I tell him, and I scoop him up off the floor.

"Oh, OK," Margaret says chuckling, "follow me," and we head down the short section of narrow hallway and into the back room that functions as both kennel and storage space.

What's a Reasonable
Price Tag for Life?

"Hey, Margaret," I answer my mobile phone. It has taken until now, 10:30 Monday morning, for me to hear from her since we departed from the clinic late Saturday afternoon.

"Hey Laura, so here's the deal, we X-rayed him first thing this morning, and I just got done looking at them. As we know, he's had massive trauma to the right hip, and basically, that femur is just banging around in there because the hip socket that the ball fits into is no longer intact. So........." she trails off for a moment, and I can hear her catching her breath. "He needs what's called a femoral head ostectomy or FHO surgery. That's where the head, and in his case, also the neck of the femur is removed."

"Will he be able to walk on that leg again?" I ask her.

"Well, that's the idea. Otherwise we'd just amputate the leg now," she replies a little testily, and we may end up having to do that anyway, but it would be nice if he could keep the leg."

"Is this surgery something you do, or would he have to go over to Michigan State?"

"No, I can do it...........I think," she chuckles, "It's not like I'm gonna hurt the leg," and she snorts and laughs some more. "He should have never been left this long," she says, in a suddenly serious tone, "the more time that transpires between the trauma and the surgery, the tougher it is. This is an anatomically difficult surgery to do anyway. Now we're working on a dog that's in a compromised body condition with calcification and scar tissue starting to develop. Does this dog have a name?"

"I named him Louie," I answer back.

"Ok. Well, we pulled some blood for labs, so as soon as Louie's bloodwork is completed, we'll be ready. I'll probably start on him in an hour or so…. Any questions?" she asks almost as an afterthought. I know that she is already in the process of closing off the outside world, and soon the only thing that will exist in her consciousness will be a buttercup yellow dog laying on a stainless steel operating table.

"I can make payments, right?" I ask with mild trepidation.

"I'm not worried about that right now," she says dismissively.

"Cool, then I'm not worried about it now either."

"I'll call you when I'm done, ok?" Margaret is ready to wrap up this conversation. "Oh yippee," she adds sarcastically, "They just handed me a positive heartworm test."

"Of course he is," I say, matching her sarcasm.

"Don't worry, he'll be fine."

"I'm not worried," I tell her. "I know he's in the best possible hands. I'll just wait until I hear from you. Good Luck, Margaret!"

"I'll need it," she snorts again and hangs up.

The Meeting

"A month is long enough," I mutter.

Dawn is arriving in shadowy, muted tones of black and grey. The dense, rain-filled clouds overhead make daybreak look more like the work of a giant eraser on heavy pencil. The minutes passing by are not making the morning bright, just less dark. I get another full body shiver and decide to continue to the barn. The clatter of rain hitting the canopy of leaves overhead completely drowns out the sound of my footsteps. Today I move slowly and carefully. My breathing is shallow, and my heart rate picks up a bit as I near the opening. As I break the plane of the doorway and pause inside the threshold, I reach inside the pocket of my jacket and gently pull out a small flashlight. I depress the button that turns on the flashlight but keep the beam pointed down toward my feet. There is a slight tremor in my hand.

"Eeeeasy girl," I say out loud.

I am amused that I am using my best horse trainer voice, low and slow, on myself. I continue holding the flashlight down where it is illuminating a circle of worn wooden floor and dried, curled-up leaves. I know that she is in the barn with me. I can sense her presence in this space and already feel the energetic contact we have made.

"And easy girl, to you, too" I say again quietly, turning my head in the direction of the ancient, musty, straw mow.

"Whoosh," I let the air rush out of my body.

"We're gonna take this very …..*very* slow, sweet pea." I turn my body, one foot at a time, until I am square with the low wall. I have to remind myself to take another breath.

"This probably seems a little rude," I say, projecting my voice toward the mow, "I just want to get an idea of where you're at, since you know exactly where I am. It's just a light, girl, nothing's gonna hurt you."

I raise the beam of light, starting low, at the bottom of the wall and slowly move it upward in a sweeping pattern side to side.

"It's just a light, girl, nothing more…...just a light," I say over and over, raising the beam a little higher with every pass.

My mind flits to a memory of my first grandson when he was about three years old. He would arrive at our house, sit on the couch with his favorite dog and coo to her, "I'm right here, Dulcey, you're fine. I'm always right here."

The memory of his sweetness makes me sigh. I blink myself back to the present and continue my search.

My heart skips a beat when the light makes a pass over something other than straw. There is a slight bouncing in the beam of light as I move my trembling hand back toward the right until the lump comes into view again. It is a dog. I immediately move the light so that it is not shining on her face, but I keep the beam positioned on the body so that I can gather a few long-awaited details. She is curled up in a tight ball and partially hidden by the depth of her makeshift nest. She appears to be of medium size, definitely not a small breed dog, but she doesn't look huge either. She is brown, but my flashlight isn't strong enough to gather much more than that.

"I'll tell you what we're gonna do......." I say, trailing off. I rest my left leg against the wooden wall and press into it, testing to see if it feels sturdy enough to support me. Slowly, I lift my left foot over and then pause, straddling the wall. I reposition the hazy beam of light back toward her body to see if my advance has caused any change. She has not moved. I proceed with lifting my right leg over, and gently lower my weight down on top of the wall. I keep my heels butted up against the wooden base in case I have gauged incorrectly, and the wall gives way, or I need to stand up quickly.

"I'm just gonna sit here with you, and we can share our first sunrise," I pause to see if any inspiring thoughts would like to show up.

"Admittedly I have no idea where we go from here. How about I call up some help.......for both of us," I say, reassuringly.

I close my eyes and take another deep breath. "St. Francis, you're the first one that comes to mind," I say out loud. "I'm asking you to join us in this space and bless this meeting with your love and light. Please share your presence here and the gifts you mastered that made all the animals feel safe and loved. Please help this lonely girl understand that I mean her no harm. I appreciate the help. Amen."

I am quiet for a moment. The only noise is the sound of the rain. I glance up toward the missing section of roof and can see the subtle changes in the color of the sky.

"It won't be long now, girl, and we will have a face to face introduction." I feel a little flutter in my stomach as I click off the flashlight and return it to my jacket pocket. I relax a little and allow my legs to slide out in front of my body.

"I'm calling Archangel Michael and Archangel Gabriel, and…..crap! I suck at names," I sigh. "I'm so sorry to you other Archangels, I need your help too, please, I just can't remember all of your names. So, just to be clear, I'm calling for help to all of the Archangels. Please share your gifts of love and light and bravery with us this morning. Please bless this meeting and keep us both safe." I can't help but notice my request has a slightly pleading quality to it.

"And fairies," I add. "We need your help too. This is an open invitation to all the white nature spirits. We need a spiritual pep rally this morning!"

Carried away in the moment, I hold my fists up in the air like I'm shaking pom-poms. But I stop dead, hands still held out to my sides, when I look up toward the now softly-lit hay mow, and a pair of eyes are locked on me.

I slowly lower my hands until they are pressed, palms together against my mouth and thumbs under my chin, like I am praying. There is suddenly a lump in my throat.

"Oh-my-gosh," I whisper into my fingers, tears instantly springing into my eyes. "You're a boxer," I say out loud, my voice sounding incredulous. For a moment we just stare, taking each other in. I lower my hands and overlap them over my heart, palms pressing into my chest and lean forward, "You're a beautiful, brindle boxer."

Don't Tell Me, Show Me

"Come on girl, let's go home." I am trying to sound enthusiastic. I am standing up gently patting my thighs with the palm of my hands.

This tactic has worked for me in the past with other dog encounters, but she isn't making a move. I turn around and make a show of filling up the two empty dog bowls with food and water. I think I detect a momentary waffle in her resolve to ignore me, but it lasts only a second or two.

"Not quite as hungry as you were thirty days ago, are you, sweetie?" I say and sit back down.

"Come on girl, let's eat!" I extend my hand holding the food dish and rattle the dry food around. She refuses to look at the bowl. I don't think she trusts either one of us.

"Oh, come on. I can start a stampede in my house with that suggestion." But she continues to ignore my pleadings.

She glances back over when I stand up. I habitually tap the left pocket of my jacket to confirm the existence of my cell phone.

"This is definitely the most awkward first date I've ever had," I say, while my right hand reaches into the other pocket and draws out a slip leash. "How about you, girl?

I am smiling as I look back toward her, but my smile fades instantly when I look at her face. Her eyes are darting now, back and forth between the leash in my hands and her surroundings. There is a look of terror in her eyes. I realize instantly that she is frantically searching for a way to get away from me.

"Oh, dear God," I moan piteously. My stomach and heart clench simultaneously. For a moment it is so hard to breathe. I feel as though I've had the wind knocked out of me.

"Oh, my God I'm an idiot. Clearly, I'm an idiot," I say, more to myself than to her. I wad the leash up in my fist and cram it back into my jacket pocket.

"I owe you an apology," I say, settling myself back down on the low wall, once again my eyes brimming with tears.

I hold my empty hands out, palms toward her. "I'm so, so sorry. This doesn't feel anything like a date to you, does it girl?"

I have made a strategic error. I feel stupid and remorseful. What the hell did I think was going to happen? That she was going to jump up, scamper down the mow, tail wagging and stick her head in the leash?

"Ugh," I groan. "Damn that one-window perspective."

I take a minute to really examine the interior of the barn. I quickly come to the conclusion that the way I came in is the only way out. I look back to where the dog is burrowed in. She has laid her head back down in a resting position, but her eyes are still worried and searching. I pull my leather work gloves off and set them down next to me. Slowly, I reach into my left coat pocket and wrap my hand around my cell phone.

"Hello," my mother answers brightly.

"Hey," is my one syllable response.

"Hi, honey, any luck today with the dog?" she asks.

"I'm sitting inside the barn with her now. She didn't get out because she never heard me coming through the woods because of the rain."

"Oh my gosh how exciting," my mom responds. "Do we need to do anything with her?"

"There's nothing to do yet. We're about fifty feet apart. She's nesting in the top of the old straw mow, and she's clearly terrified. It's an old, grey-faced boxer, Mom," I say, and the tears well up again.

"Do you want me to come over there?" my mom offers, the emotion in her voice matching the emotion in mine.

We are emotional animals, this woman and I. I have inherited two of my mother's most prominent features: we both sport the exact same large, too-big for-our-faces nose as well as our openly-displayed, ardent hearts on our sleeves.

"No. I think that would just be more upsetting," I sigh. "I'm going to have to try to get to her, Mom. Are you staying home?" I ask but don't give her time to answer.

"There's actually a huge hole in the floor. I didn't realize until today that this barn has like a basement level to it. I have no idea if the floor under the straw will support me. I'm hoping not to end up like Humpty Dumpty," I laugh nervously.

There is silence, "Mom?" I say. "Are you still there?"

"I'm not going to tell you not to do it." My mom's voice is thick, and there is another pause.

"But you need to call me every ten minutes and let me know you're ok." She is trying to sound calm and stern, and I appreciate her attempt at bravado.

"I'm not calling every ten minutes, Mom. Give me a half hour," I say, "and you call me back. On the very, off chance that I don't pick up, try me again, but if I don't pick up twice, go to the farm and get Craig. Ok, Mom?" I wait for her to reply.

"Ok," she answers. "I love you, honey. Be careful."

"You know I will. I love you too, Mom. Hey," I say quickly before she hangs up, "leave dad out of this for now, or he'll be calling me every five minutes."

"Good luck, sweetie," is her response, and she hangs up.

I click the button on my phone to check the time before sliding it back into my pocket. It is 8:07 a.m.

"Hey girl," I say directly to her, and she lifts her head and looks at me.

"I don't suppose you'd like to just walk down here so we can go home?"

Of course, I am not really expecting her to make a move, and she doesn't. She just continues to stare at me.

"I got to tell ya, you've got kind of a poker face."

Having lived and worked with animals my whole life, I consider myself a "good reader" of body language and facial expression. On numerous occasions, I have experienced what I believe to be clairsentience: the ability to feel what another sentient being is feeling. But at the moment, this girl feels shut down. She is locked and loaded in survival mode, relying completely on her primal instincts. I believe her isolation; coupled with the sheer effort of staying alive has taken the wind out of her sails. I don't sense any aggression here, but I know I am pushing her to the limit, encroaching into her private space. I can only wonder if my presence feels like salvation or persecution, 'cause she's not saying anything.

I stand up and play with the zipper on my jacket, contemplating my next move.

"I'm coming to you, girl. I don't see any other way to handle this."

I take a few tentative steps toward the straw mow, never letting my eyes leave her face. She tracks my movement with wide-open, bloodshot eyes. I can see her pressing her body weight down into the cubbyhole she has created in the straw. She is desperately trying to make herself disappear. Slowly, I reach back in my pockets and pull out my leather gloves.

"No leash here, girlie. I'm just gonna put these back on."

I speak to her as slowly as I'm moving. Once the gloves are back on my hands, I bend my knees and squat down, palms on the floor and sit on my butt at the base of the straw mow.

"Just for the record, I feel vulnerable too," I tell her. "We've only sort of known each other a month now, but I already love you. Do you hear me, girl?" and as I ask the question, something in the tone of my voice makes her raise her head and look at me.

"I love you," I say again.

I press my palms down on each side of my hips and lift my rear end slightly off the ground. Moving one hand at a time, and one foot at a time, I walk myself backwards until I have traveled a foot or two. Even this almost immeasurable distance has caused her fear to intensify. I can see her body is quivering as if she is cold.

"It's ok, girl. There's still a lot of space between you and me. We're gonna take our time and get to know each other." I renew my resolve to stay calm and relaxed.

I Will Get the Last
Word......Shocker!

The family spends the day going through several extremely well organized family photo albums my mother had spent years compiling, with dates and names on the back of most pictures. This exercise in family history has provided a much needed interval of laughter and camaraderie that reminds all of us that we are still intrinsically connected to each other, even though the strongest link in our familial chain has broken away from us. Everyone at the condo goes through the photos, but it ends up being the girls of the family who put the photo boards together that will be displayed at the funeral home the following day. I think it is my sister who suggests three boards chronicling our mother's life. Again, we are all in agreement.

Later in the evening, just after the dinner hour, the minister from the Methodist church my parents attend arrives at the condominium. The entire family is still here. He is meticulous about recording everyone's name and relationship to my mom and directs several questions to the group designed to solicit both conversation and information about my mother's life. Despite his obvious expertise in this type of emotionally-charged situation, I find him annoying. His demeanor is very polished and his speech very measured, but to me it feels laced with arrogance. When his time with us draws to a close, he asks if anyone in the family would be interested in speaking at my mother's funeral, and I can feel everyone in the room recoil at the mere thought of it. They are either mute, gazing at the floor, or shaking their heads "no." I raise my hand. The minister looks at me and then looks down to consult his copious notes, "And you're Laura, correct?" he asks me, in his patronizing tone and makes a gesture my way.

"Yep," I say and nod my head.

"Oh, you should, mom," says my daughter. "Someone should speak for the family." And now, several heads are bobbing in agreement.

"I will certainly try," is all I say. I have absolutely no idea of what I will say or whether or not I will even be capable of standing at my mother's funeral and uttering a coherent word, but it feels important.

Group Therapy

I think we are all relieved that for the first time in almost twelve months; I am no longer the neediest member of the pack. Louie's arrival home has given all of us something to focus on. His complete dependency and vulnerability will instantly reaffirm the pecking order of the pack. When I carry him into the house on Tuesday afternoon, the ensuing scuttle of activity looks like actors dashing around on stage, assuming assigned positions to set the scene of a play. But instead of me placing this tragic and forlorn-looking dog on the folded comforter in the middle of the kitchen floor and clapping my hands shouting, "places, everyone," I set him there as an offering to the pack and back away saying, "let the healing begin."

They are immediately aware that Louie poses no threat. They would have come to that conclusion quickly without the injury, just based on his inherently kind nature, but it is immediately evident to them, and even to me, with my dull human senses, that his level of life energy is low. I squat down and join the group on the floor with him, reaching out to stroke his head, "Now that life has kicked the shit out of both of us, and we've survived, I suggest we get on with living," I tell him, "I'm what's called a facilitator. They're the experts," I say, acknowledging the other dogs gathered around, "they're gonna show you how it's done."

After a few hours of lying on the floor, I know I have to force Louie to get up. Even if his bladder isn't full, Margaret's instructions were crystal clear: "As much as he's been through, Laura, if you don't make him get up, he may just lay there and die. Like any surgery, you have to force the body away from the anesthesia, and *he has to move*. He's going to need encouragement to live," she added somberly.

"So, here's the deal, buddy," I say, squatting down again in front of him, "it's called rehab. I'm pretty sure you're not going to want to participate at first, but we're kinda big on survival here. We're gonna help you heal, inside and out, buttercup. We're your pack now."

When I make my move to pick him up off the floor, all of the other dogs gather around. The anticipated maneuver has captured their interest. Up to this point, their only perspective of him has been a listless mass in the middle of the kitchen floor. "I think a little fresh air will do you a world of good, buddy. You haven't been outside in……. geez, almost two weeks. That ain't healthy, Lou. Up we go," I tell him, straddling him from the top and gently rolling his weight off the left side of his body, far enough for me to slide my hand under his prominent rib cage. My hold on him has shifted him up slightly on his sternum. He isn't fighting me, but he isn't helping me either. "On three, buddy, one…two…three." I squeeze my eyes partially closed in anticipation of him possibly responding to pain inflicted by the movement. The effort produces only a low groan, and I can't say for sure which one of us it escapes from.

"Look at you standing up," I say to him. My fingers are laced together so my arms are acting like a sling under his ribs, and my legs on either side of him are stabilizing his very unstable back-end. His right rear leg is dangling uselessly. "From up here, your incision looks like a smile; we'll take that as a sign," I tell him, bending forward and planting a kiss on the top of his head.

"Come on, Lou, we got some ground to cover before we hit grass, so let's get going." I begin by scooting my feet and pressing my hands against his ribs to shift his weight. I can feel him resist slightly, but he is much too weak and unstable to put up much of a fight. He takes a hesitant move forward, something between a hop and a shuffle. "Good boy," I coo from over the top of his head, "what a good boy,"" and so it goes for the next ten to fifteen minutes as we scoot-shuffle-hop our way toward the back door. We navigate the galley-shaped laundry room and arrive at the back door. Beyond the door is a ten-foot square deck with five steps that lead to a good-sized fenced-in yard. We pause before opening the door, and I reach up and grab one of my husband's jackets hanging on a metal hook. It feels good to stand up straight. As I work the coat around my back, I crouch slightly and support the dog by gently squeezing him between my knees and thighs. "The dog succeeds where so many men have failed," I laugh out loud. "Alright, buddy, we're almost there," I tell him, stretching my right hand forward and opening the door. He stands still for a moment, taking in the view but then clumsily lurches forward, eager to get outside.

"Whoa, buddy," I take a few stiff-legged steps, still straddling him over the threshold. It sounds like a hose has been turned on. He is frozen in place and peeing. The warm urine is splashing against the slushy, snow-covered deck boards with so much force, we are both getting splattered. I stand still too, waiting for his bladder to empty. I have never seen a dog urinate for this long. "Holy shit, dude, that's what I call potty trained! You must have been ready to burst." I swing my leg over him and stand close so he can lean against me, and I stroke the length of his back. "I'm gonna carry you down the steps," I explain, "you need a little yard time, Dr. Margaret's orders."

Once out in the yard, he drops his nose instantly to the ground, inhaling the diverse, multifold scents as only a dog can. His instincts have him taking one and then two shaky steps forward. His effort is rewarded as the other dogs gather, sharing their moist noses to enhance the aromas. "Good for you," I whisper, standing a few feet away watching the scene in front of me, shaking my head up and down. "You have just rediscovered your dogness. Good for you." I take a few steps away, and the other dogs immediately move to follow me, curious to see why I am touring their yard. "Come on, Lou. Come check it out with us." He wants to follow. I can see it in his soft, Milk Dud-colored eyes, but he can't. *I'm exhausted*, his expression says.

"I suppose now that your bladder doesn't feel like it's going to explode, you would probably like to rest," and I walk back over to where he is standing and scoop him up. "Ok, boy, we'll try again in a few hours."

At bedtime, I am indecisive, and Louie is melancholy. "I've been under anesthesia and had body parts removed," I tell him, "that hangover is a bitch, isn't it, buddy?" He is unmoved by my commiserative disclosure. "Alright, Lou, you sleep it off for now, and we'll pick this back up in the morning," I tell him, clicking off the kitchen light and heading upstairs, seven dogs on my heels. The large dogs settle down, cozied into one of the several beds on the floor.

The three small dogs grumble at one another and jockey for what they believe is the coveted spot on our bed. I've never figured that out. By morning, they will all three be huddled together like newborn puppies. I shove two little bodies off my pillow, climb in and pull the bedding over my legs. Otis is already huddled under the covers and growls softly, just so I know he doesn't appreciate being disturbed. "Way to be grateful, Otis," I say, swatting the lump. Suddenly I flip off the covers, swing my legs over and stand back up. Kaya is instantly on her feet too. "I can't do this," I say, exasperated.

"Can't do what?" mumbles Denny, dozing off in his usual position: sitting up, chin to his chest and his book dangling off the side of his lap.

"I can't leave him down there alone....on the floor......in the dark," I am yelling now from halfway down the stairs, Kaya following close behind.

"Then leave a light on," I hear him yell after me.

"Gosh, you're so smart. Why didn't I think of that?" I say with sunshiny sarcasm.

"I can hear you," he yells.

"I can hear you too," I volley back.

"So, how ya doing, Lou?" I ask the yellow dog as I bend down to stroke his head.

"What?" Denny's voice carries down the open vent that's behind the headboard of our bed and is open to the kitchen.

"Not you, Denny," I yell back.

I am farm-girl strong, so it is more awkward than strenuous for me to carry Lou up the narrow farmhouse staircase. I secure my footing one step at a time and keep my back pressed against the wall that lacks a handrail for additional support. Kaya silently follows behind. Only once, when attempting to look beyond his body to scrutinize our progress do I bump his nose into the wall. I enter the room and look directly at the sleeping figure sitting in the bed and decide silence is my best strategy. I set Louie down in the margin of space between the wall and the side rails of our giant king-sized bed. He seems content with my placement of him, so I climb back in my side, and before I turn my light off, I notice Kaya settle herself down in the small, open area on the floor next to Louie. She is the beta dog to Rose's matriarchal alfa, and like most seconds-in-command, does the majority of the work. I smile and tap my bedside light off.

"So, you're gonna carry that dog up and down the stairs every day?" I hear Denny ask me in the dark.

"No, I'm just making sure he knows he's part of this family, and we love him, so he has a reason to want to walk up and down the stairs himself," I say.

It's quiet for a moment, and all I can hear is the furnace running and Rose's soft snoring. "I love you," Denny says.

"I love you back," I tell him.

This is our routine for the next three or four days. Louie's post-surgical appetite is negligible. Twice a day, while the other dogs are also eating, I hand feed him out of a bowl while sitting next to him on his blanket. Every few hours I assist him up and to the door, or at least part of the way to the door before scooping him up and carrying him. I always set him down at the bottom of the steps so he can pee in the yard, and I always set him in front of the water dish in the laundry room once we are back inside. He is a voracious drinker. More and more I am leaving him unattended at the water bowl to make his own way back to his spot on the kitchen floor.

Gratitude

Louie still looks exhausted, but I watch with great interest as his relationships with his housemates begin to evolve. The two that are the most attentive are Sadie, a Miniature Schnauzer we acquired from one of our daughters, and Kaya. I think Sadie's attraction to Louie is her lack of popularity due to stunted social skills and the intolerance of her overly-excitable nature from the largely senior pack. Kaya's interest, however, is selfless and driven by a sense of duty. Sadie crawls up next to his back to take advantage of his emanating body heat and fluffy comforter, while Kaya stands, or sometimes lies, face to face with him and meticulously cleans his ears and eyes with her tongue. Other than these two girls, no one has a keen interest in him, but rather his presence here is accepted and comfortable for all of us.

After a week or so of bitter cold days, the temperature finally crawls above the teens, so I put on my barn boots, jacket and gloves and prepare to spend some time out in the yard with my troupe. Once I set Louie down and stabilize him as usual, I walk away, heading toward the front of the house. As I move forward, I spend most of my time looking down to avoid the pitfalls of walking in an area dominated by well-fed dogs. My diligence in yard cleaning is admittedly dictated by the weather, and it has been bitter cold. When I finally stop moving and pick my eyes up, I have traveled thirty feet or so, and heading my way, stopping intermittently to sniff a spot of interest with the others, is the buttercup yellow dog. His leg is dangling, almost as though he has forgotten it is there, but when he lifts his head to look at me and perks his ears in response to my excited applause at his progress, for the first time, his eyes are smiling.

Spring

Early spring brings with it visible signs of re-birth and renewal, not just outside but inside as well. Louie is steadily gaining weight, and now I place his food dish in front of the stove so that he has to stand up and walk over to it. I have removed the comforter from the middle of the kitchen floor, and he and the pack spend the majority of their time on the sunporch dozing in front of the gas log fireplace. The big dogs have a daily game of musical couch cushions. The minute one of them vacates its space to go potty or get a drink, another one quickly takes over the spot. The little dogs are like a sundial, starting out the morning on the arm of the sofa, closest to the fire, and moving upward across the back of the cushions as the rays of sunshine travel west. Once the last shaft of the day is no longer streaming in through the glass, the little band of heat-seeking nomads will collectively migrate back to the beginning, to the arm of the sofa next to the fire.

I am standing at the kitchen window and watch as one of our farm workers pulls off the main road and onto our property. I can tell with a fair amount of accuracy at what point in the car's progression up the gravel drive the dogs will catch on to the arrival and dash out the door with a raucous greeting. "Wait for it.........now," I say, and with nothing more than a one or two second delay, they are off, careening around the corner of the laundry room and blasting out the dog door, barking as though their lives depended on it. What I am not expecting is the instantaneous lump that forms in my throat as I watch Louie, who must have stood up while the others were running out, ambling through the kitchen and around the corner in apparent pursuit of his pack. I let him get in front of me, and then I follow along. When he stops at the barrier of the dog door, I reach past him and push the flexible plastic curtain outward, to reveal the opening. "Go on, Lou," I encourage him, "go on, buddy. Go outside and bark," and to my amazement, he lowers his head and clumsily passes through the opening, his injured leg dragging through like an afterthought. I immediately open the door and follow him out. He has never been outside unattended. "Lou, you crafty son-of-a- bitch!" I am vigorously patting his ribcage. "You just let yourself out. I'm so proud of you." In response to my enthusiasm, he gifts me with a slow wag of his tail.

Angel is the only one still barking. She barks so vigorously her front end lifts off the top step of the deck, which is her favorite perch. She would bark for hours if I would let her, as I'm sure the neighbors would attest. I am constantly poking my head out of the end of the barn to yell, "Angel, shut up!" The other dogs have lost interest and are wandering around the yard. "As long as we're on a roll, how do you feel about tackling the steps?" I ask Louie. Another slow wag, which I interpret as a *yes*. I loop my finger under his collar and guide him to the edge of the steps. I can tell by the way he is planting himself that he is anticipating me picking him up as usual. But I don't. Instead, I move my right foot down one step, wrap my arms around his middle and slowly pull him forward until he has no choice but to step down with his front feet. I repeat the process, but he is a little more hesitant this time because the back foot has to move down onto a step. I'm sure the angle is a little unnerving, and he probably feels like he's going to fall face first at the bottom of the stairs. "Come on, boy, this will be less scary if we keep moving," I tell him. So I pull, and he steps, and before we know it, we are one step away from the bottom. Without warning, Louie leaps, literally, out of my arms and over the last wooden step. Adrenaline has my heart pounding as I watch Louie land on three legs and take a few galloping strides out into the yard. Once he stops, he turns and faces me. I am holding my breath, praying to God that he has not re-injured his surgical site, and as I stare at him, the answer to my fears becomes crystal clear. Louie is sporting the goofy grinning of an adolescent boy who has just seen his first nudie picture: surprised, a little unsure, and very pleased.

Three days a week I watch my granddaughter while her parents work. She was born two weeks after my mother died. Her emergence into this world at a time when I was reeling with grief was both a celebration and a blow to me emotionally. People were quick to share their comforting words to both me and my daughter that the woman we were desperately missing was certain to be taking all of this in from her vantage point in heaven. While I appreciate their support, and actually believe with all my heart that my mother has viewed and blessed this child, it does not change the fact that I feel cheated not to be sharing this experience with her in her human form. But this little girl is perfection, and just like my relationship with Louie, each of us pulls the other forward in life.

My granddaughter has already morphed from an infant to a toddler when Louie comes into our lives and joins our family. When she first arrives at the house, I carry her until the flurry of dog activity settles down, and we all return to our individual pursuits. A few times she has been at the rough end of the stick and been pushed, bumped and even knocked down by a dog that was inconsiderate of her size and space. But for the most part, all of the dogs are familiar and comfortable with this scaled-down human. She navigates easily among this tolerant group, and upon arrival, they indulge her in her favorite activity of poking each and every one of them on the top of the head and attempting to repeat their names as I say them. She and Lou have a love-hate relationship, and at least once per visit, she will yell and wag her tiny finger at him in an attempt to command him to stop licking her. I have no concerns with regard to her well-being. Today we are upstairs in the spare bedroom that we have converted into a playroom. Louie, who has mastered the staircase now, has been our companion in the bedroom from the beginning. When he first arrived, I would set my granddaughter down with a toy and then dash back to the bottom of the stairs, scoop up Louie and place him on the single bed so I could monitor both of my charges at the same time.

At the moment my granddaughter is dancing along with her favorite video on the TV in the corner. Every time this is on, I marvel at the ingenuity of this group of adult men dressed in primary colors, all with a negligible amount of talent, who have organized themselves into a wildly successful, money-making venture. I always feel like I need a mental shower when she leaves to clear the repetitive and ridiculously simple lyrics out of my head. Like her, I know every word and every hand gesture to every song….God help me! As I emerge from the open door of the bathroom, Lou literally pours himself off the bed, like a snake slithering off a rock. He stands to greet me in the doorway, slowly wagging his sizable tail, which is bumping my granddaughter across the back of her shoulders, whack….whack….whack, as she tries to maneuver to a song about cold spaghetti. Louie and I are both completely startled when, without any warning, she pirouettes on one tiny, sock-clad foot, grabs his tail with both of her hands, and bites down. "No, no, no," I grab his tail away with one hand and her arm with the other. When she unclenches her jaw and looks up at me, a serious and self-righteous expression in her crystal blue eyes, I am instantly moved to gut-wrenching laughter: her tiny lips are coated with white and yellow hairs. "Little princess," I chuckle, "you look like you've eaten a rabbit."

The Truth, The Whole Truth, and Nothing but the Truth So Help Me God.

I gaze toward the roof of the barn at nothing in particular and say, "I trust you spirits are doing your part to help her understand what's happening here."

I let out a long, slow breath and move myself up the gradual slope of the mow another foot or two then settle my weight back down.

"I'd like to tell you a true story." I pause to mull over my willingness to go where this topic will take me.

"This'll be the first time I've ever shared this story," I say, looking up at her and pausing again.

"I've spent a lot of years telling myself to forget about it, that life is a forward- moving experience, but it seems fitting under the circumstances, and it appears we've got plenty of time. If at any time you want me to shut up, feel free to get up and come put your paw over my mouth." I pause and look up at her.

"I feel compelled to tell you, I'm long winded and cry at the drop of a hat…..and at some point, you're gonna meet my mom, and I guarantee when she finally gets to meet you, she'll be crying too." Her head is back down, jowls resting on the edge of her makeshift nest.

"First off, I want to say 'thank you' for the past twenty-nine days. It's been awhile since I've stretched my emotional wings. Thank you for so graciously allowing me into your life. Thank you for letting me see myself in you. Thank you for sharing my evolution. I understand you're probably feeling very threatened and uncertain where this is going. Despite my earlier misconception that you would be as excited to meet me as I was to meet you, I have a pretty good idea of how you're feeling right now." I sigh and grab an old piece of straw off the floor and run it through my gloved fingers, making a series of kinks in it before tossing it aside.

"It is incredibly stupid for me to think this situation holds any of the 'butterfly belly' anticipation of a first date." I pick up another shaft of straw and repeat the process of running it through my fingers.

"I actually have first-hand knowledge of the terror that comes with being a hostage." I pause and stare at the space between my shoes.

"I believe that's the reason we're in this barn together." I sigh and absently grab another piece of old, faded straw.

"That day changed my view of the world." My throat is tight, and tears are already brimming in my eyes. "It changed my life." I gaze up at her, and for a moment, we just look at each other. "This day will change our lives too."

"I'm gonna move a little closer so you can hear me," I say in a conversational tone. Using the same action, I lift my butt up again and walk myself back another few feet and begin to tell her my story:

"So, there was this beautiful soul that needed a lift down to earth. Apparently, I had agreed, before my incarnation here, that I would be her portal into this lifetime. Part of her journey and mine was that we would be mother and daughter. That's my favorite part of this story." I glance up at the dog to make my point.

"Well, in order for her to make her entrance into the world to start her journey, and for me to continue with mine, I apparently needed to meet and marry her father in a whirlwind romance. While I appreciated the incredible gift of my daughter, it became apparent to me almost immediately that her conception and birth was the best thing that was going to happen between me and her father. Our life threads were not meant to be any more or any less entwined than that. Although the day-to-day experience of ending that relationship was tumultuous most of the time, I wanted to be past it so desperately I just kept moving myself toward that goal. My grandmother, my mother's-mother, was my greatest ally at the time. We spent hours every week visiting and talking on the phone. Her blunt, matter-of-fact personality, along with her financial support, provided a huge safety net for me."

"Speaking of safety nets….." As if on cue, the phone in my pocket starts ringing. I pull the glove off my right hand and press the button to pick up the call.

"Hey, Mom," I answer.

"How are things going with the dog?" my mom asks brightly.

"It goes," I say in response to her question. "Call back in another thirty minutes or so," I tell her, and we both hang up.

I place my phone back in my pocket and stare for a moment at the dog in her nest. In response to my stare, she raises her head and stares back at me.

"I told you, if you're tired of hearing me talk, then you need to come down here, and I'll be quiet."

I place my hands behind my back again and raise my weight up so I can scoot myself a few more feet in her direction. Her eyes dart nervously from side to side, but other than that she remains motionless in her nest.

"So, where was I?" I ask the dog, picking up another piece of straw to fidget with.

"Oh yeah, beautiful daughter, crappy marriage, blah, blah, blah. Unlike you, my lovely lady, it wouldn't dawn, until many years later, that I should rescue myself.

"The details of my marital situation may have been unique, but I don't think the essence of the failure was. I realize now that my attraction for him was actually a complicated and elaborate distraction away from myself. I was hoping our relationship would somehow magically transport me away from the messy housekeeping of my life that I had deemed either too painful or too embarrassing to acknowledge. And, while self-doubt, avoidance and addiction was driving my bus, my brain went on a fantasy-filled, emotional holiday, crafting a romantic fairytale that was destined to quickly crumble.

"Relationship failure was the absolute best possible outcome. It propelled me forward in my life, now with a child at my side, with re-shuffled priorities and several new notations on my "'What I Don't Want in My Life' list."

I stop talking and sigh. "Headed your way, darlin'," I tell her and scoot myself several feet closer toward her perch. She watches me closely but still doesn't move her body, except for the almost spasm-like, intermittent shivering.

"I can see you're overwhelmed with anticipation, waiting to hear the rest of my story." I make a derisive snort. I scoot my body another foot or so and glance across the barn. My eyes pass over the hole in the floor, and I reflexively tap the pocket that holds my cell phone.

"So, have you heard the one about the lady, the toddler and the neighbor kid that walk in on a jewelry store robbery? Well, it wasn't actually a joke. It's funny, though, how such a small segment of time has the ability to change us so significantly." I pause, letting my mind float back over recollections of those days, "There's a whole lot of dust on those memories."

"I don't even remember how I got the idea to pawn my wedding ring. It's not like I needed the money. I think it was more an act of rebellion. The final, 'screw you, I'm outta here!' But, when I left the YMCA that morning, walked across the street clad in a leotard and tights, a toddler on my hip and holding hands with the beautiful little redheaded seven-year-old who lived in the house next door to me, in a matter of minutes, on what started out as a perfectly normal summer weekday, I was the one who was screwed.

"I sensed danger the second I walked in. Maybe the second before I walked in. I pressed down on the lever-style door handle and pushed the door open. There was a moment when time literally held still, and several of us were momentarily stunned as I stood on the threshold. Me, trying to process what I was seeing, and the thieves because someone had forgotten to lock the front door. Just as the thought, "GET OUT!" was screaming in my head, a tall, thin man, his features distorted by the pressure from the nylon stocking over his face and a gun in one hand took a quick, firm hold of my upper right arm. I immediately dropped my head down and cast my eyes at the floor. Reflexively I pressed my daughters' head tight against my breasts and wrapped my arm around the little redheaded girl, drawing her in tight against my body, the palm of my hand covering her eyes.

"'I'm sorry ma'am, you and the kids are gonna have to stay here.' The tall gunman says, pulling me inside the store. I think my heart has literally stopped beating as he pulls my rigid body further into the store.

"'Stop,' he tells me when we are a few feet inside.

"He maneuvers behind me toward the door and releases his grasp on my arm, but our connection is quickly replaced as he firmly presses what I realize is a gun barrel into my back. I flinch and suck in a quick breath of air.

'Don't move,' he says, and I hear the door lock click.

"My reaction has frightened my little companion. She is frantically trying to pull my hand away from her face. I move my right hand up and press the baby into my body as I bend down and lean over the child pressing my mouth into her hair.

"'Shhhhh, honey. I want you to put your arms around me and stay right next to me. Don't let go of me no matter what. Don't let go of me.' I repeat adamantly, and I feel her tiny arms move around and squeeze my hips.

"The gunman is back on my right side. He is clutching my upper arm with what feels like a huge claw. His large hand and long, thin fingers feel like an iron cuff, completely encircling my bicep. He is pulling me toward the end of a long, glass case filled with jewelry that runs down the long side of the shoebox-shaped store.

"'Get down back here,' he says, pointing his gun in the narrow space between the wall and the backside of the case. 'Keep your eyes down. Don't let me catch you looking up.'

"I take small, shuffling, sideways steps. My right hand is still pressing my daughter against my shoulder and chest, and my left hand is over the eyes of the now, very frightened and whimpering little redhead. I press her face into my stomach."

The dog and I are both startled when my phone rings. She pops her head up and stares at me. It takes my mind a second or two to get back to where I am: sitting in a musty straw mow. I pull off my glove and fish my phone out of my pocket. I don't bother with "Hello."

"Hey. I'm not there yet, Mom, but I'm close." My tone is slightly clipped. Perhaps sensing something in my voice, my mom repeats her earlier offer.

"You're sure you don't want me there? I could just stand by and watch," she says.

"No, Mom. We're just getting acquainted. Another person, even one as sweet as you, would be a disruption at this point." I am consciously relaxing my tone.

"O.K., honey." There is a pause, and I sense that she wants to say something else but doesn't. "I'll check back in a bit."

"Thank you, Mom. I'm sure you have other things you could be doing today."

"Nothing as important as this," she replies and hangs up.

"So, where was I?" I ask the dog, after I return my phone to my jacket pocket and pulled my glove back on.

"Oh, that's right, heading behind the jewelry counter." I absently reach down and pick up another piece of straw.

"The children and I move like we are velcroed together. After maybe five or six steps down the wall, heading toward the back of the store and away from the front door, the tall gunman says, 'Right there. Get down right there.'

"*Get down how?* I'm wondering. "*I can't lay down with these two kids*"

Irritated with my indecision, he barks at me, 'I said sit down!'

"*You said 'get down' you mother-fucker, not 'sit down,'* my voice is screaming in my head.

"I pull both children tight against me and slide my body down the wall. When my weight starts to pull the little redhead down, she resists and starts to cry.

"'Sit down,' I hiss at her.

"'Noooo,' she cries and is writhing frantically trying to break my hold on her.

"I muscle her down to the floor with me. My back is against the wall, and my knees are pulled up, feet against the base of the long jewelry counter. I pull the baby across my lap so she is facing me, straddling my lap with my right arm around her back and adjust my hold on the terrified child sitting next to me. My left arm is around her waist under her left arm, and the palm of my hand is pressing against her chest, her head tucked up against my shoulder. Her hands feel like claws clutching tight on my forearm, her little fingernails digging into the surface of my skin.

'I want my mommy,' she half moans and half cries.

'I know you want your mommy, honey,' I whisper into the top of her head, my mouth making contact with her hair, 'and when we get home, she's gonna give you a big hug and kiss, but right now, sweetie, you need to do exactly what I tell you. Your momma wants you to do *exactly* what I tell you.'

She is still for a moment, but I do not loosen my grip on her. My eyes are still cast down. When I shift my gaze to the floor space to the right of me, I notice for the first time that there is a body of a woman lying on the floor to the right of where we are sitting. She is face down on her belly. I can hear her stressed breathing.

"The robbers are talking. I know that there are at least two of them, the one who grabbed my arm and the one who was pulling items out of the case identical to the one I am sitting behind on the opposite side of the store. I caught a glimpse of him when I walked in. I can't believe this is happening downtown in broad daylight.

"'Momma, momma,' my daughter's tiny hands are trying to lift my chin so I will look at her.

'Hey beautiful girl,' I pull her forward towards my chest. 'Just sit still with mommy.' She is tipping her tiny head sideways and pushing my forehead with the soft little palms of her hands, trying to press my head up so she can see my face.

"My interaction with the baby has aroused the redhead from what is probably shock-induced silence. I feel her brace against me and then try to twist her body the other direction, momentarily unlocking her death-grip on my arm and attempting to crawl away from me, presumably toward the door.

"'No, no, no, no, no, sweetie,' I flex my arm, and in one motion I have pulled her back into me, smashing her back tightly against the crook of my left shoulder.

"'No sweetie, no sweetie, don't do that. You have to stay with me, honey, right here against me,' I am murmuring the words into her hair.

"'I want my mommy, I want to go hooooome,' she cries desperately while digging and scratching her tiny fingernails across the skin of my forearm, her feet kicking frantically at the base of the counter in front of us.

"'Shhhh sweetie. Stop that,' I say firmly into her hair and drop my left leg against hers in an attempt to stop her from kicking.

"'I know you want to go home. We're gonna go home real soon. Do you pray at school, honey?' I ask her, sounding almost frantic remembering that she goes to the Catholic elementary school.

"'Do you pray at school?' I prompt her again and feel a slight nod of her head. 'Because that's what God and your mommy want you to do while you're sitting here with me. They want you to sit very still and pray and tell God all the things in your life that you like the best. Pray really quiet, sweetie, in your head. Tell God about your favorite food, and your favorite toys and your favorite TV show and what you want to be when you grow up.'

"'Get up,' I hear a deep, demanding voice say, and my blood literally runs cold. 'You too,' he says. 'Both of you get up.'

"I can hardly breathe any air in, my chest is so tight. My eyes are locked open, and I am searching the floor trying to figure out where he is standing. I hear the shuffling of movement and realize he is not talking to me. There are other hostages that I cannot see.

"Which one of you owns the store?' I hear the gunman ask. I have surmised that he is the one in charge.

"'I do,' I hear a man's voice answer quietly.

"'Where are the coins and the diamonds?' he demands. There is a moment of silence.

"Don't fuck with me, man, where are the fucking coins and diamonds?" He asks again. He must have raised his gun because the store owner begins to spit out his response is a series of verbal trips and halts.

"'In, in, in the safe….and mu-mu-most of the coins are, um, the coins are, um, downstairs…in the basement.'

"'Go,' says the gunman, 'both of you, downstairs.'

"'No, please,' I hear a man's shaky voice softly pleading. I recognize that this is another man, not the shop owner.

"'Shut up and do what you're told,' the gunman says. 'Go, now.'

"I hear the frightened man moan, and then footsteps descending the stairs. I believe the frightened man and I are thinking the same thing: that we will all end up in the basement dead.

"My daughter has had enough of her confinement. 'Go mommy, go mommy,' she is whining, bouncing her body up and down on my lap and pulling at the front of my leotard.

"'Hush, baby girl,' I whisper to her and pull her toward my chest. 'Be momma's good girl, you be momma's good girl, and when we leave here, I'll take you to the park.

"'No mommy, no mommy, no mommy.' She is getting worked up and fighting against my grip on her. Her little palms are pressing against my breasts, and her body is rigid in a frustrated attempt to push herself away from me. When I do not loosen my hold, she begins rocking her body back and forth between my chest and my knees. Being wedged in this small space is fueling her frustration, and she is throwing herself backwards toward the jewelry case. I clutch the back of her little summer shirt and wad the fabric in the tight grip of my fist so I can control her upper body, and she cannot tumble out of my arm. She is bawling now.

The second I sense footsteps to the right of me, he is already talking. I have not heard this voice before. There are three of them. I clamp my arms tighter around both of the girls' bodies.

"He has stepped over the top of the woman on the floor, and I hear her moan in fear. 'Shut that fuckin' kid up, do you hear me, bitch?' I wince when he thumps the hard steel of his gun barrel into the side of my head.

"'If you don't shut that fuckin' kid up,' he says bending over us, 'I'm gonna blow her fucking head off in your lap.' His tone is taunting and excited. He is close enough that I can smell his bad breath. As if to prove his point, he presses the end of his gun barrel up against my daughter's tiny blonde head.

"'Oh dear God,' the woman on the floor moans.

"'Shut the fuck up, old lady,' he kicks his foot backwards towards her body, and I hear her terrified groan.

I am clutching my daughter so tightly I am afraid I will break her. I roll my right shoulder forward and try to hide her underneath my body and next to the little redhead. I pull both girls against me as tightly as possible and turn my back to him in an attempt to shield them. One or both of them is whimpering. 'Hush, baby girl, hush, baby girl,' I say frantically, over and over.

"'Get back over there,' a deep voice commands. This is the voice of the man who was leaning over the jewelry case when I walked in. My eyes are closed, and I try to focus on the man I can still hear breathing behind me. *Walk away, walk away, walk away*, I am willing him. Another forceful punch to the side of my head and he says, 'Fuck you, bitch.'

"I have two distinct impressions after that. The first is a warm, spreading sensation under my hip and thigh, and for a moment I think that I must have missed the part when he shot me. My mind is frantically trying to recall a gunshot or feel the bullet. Had I passed out? Oh dear God, had he shot my daughter? And then I hear the little redhead, muffled under my body: 'I wet my pants,' she says in a tiny, anguished voice.

"'It's ok, sweetie," I whisper. I am making a manic, rocking motion with my body in an attempt to comfort all of us. 'It's ok,' I say again trying to soothe this traumatized child. 'I think I wet my pants too, sweetheart. It's ok, honey. Its ok if we wet our pants.'

"'Shut up, bitch,' I am told again by the man with the excitable tone. He is intoxicated on our fear.

'Go fuck yourself.' I mouth the words without any sound, hatred for this man boiling up inside of me. And then, like someone turning off a light switch, my rage is gone. I am saturated in an ineffable sense of deep, deep peace. I am literally and completely untethered from the terror of my situation. The Universe has sent me a gift, the gift of complete and total acceptance. I am, in that moment, completely free of fear or struggle. In the midst of this nightmare, a beautiful moment has arrived. God is sitting right here next to me, and I am immersed in the absolute

peace of his presence. Looking back, I realize that gift was sent to me as a reference point, a beacon that I would need to remember as I headed into the biggest battle of my life, my battle to save myself.

"I press my head down so that I can feel both girls faces against my cheeks, 'This little light of mine, I'm gonna let it shine….' I whisper the same verse over and over. If this song has more words to it, I have no idea what they are."

When I stop talking and look up at the dog, I let out a soft laugh. I have caught her in the long, slow blinking of dozing off.

"I see you have succumbed to my company in your barn, and are obviously under impressed with my mastery of the monologue," I chide her. "You can't say I didn't warn you about being long winded."

I take advantage of her relaxed state and make a few big advances in her direction. I have closed the gap by more than half now. She intently monitors my progress. This time, she raises her head slightly, and I see her eyes search the space beyond where I am sitting, toward the barn door. I notice for the first time how old and tired she looks.

"No, sweetie" I tell her, "Please don't think bolting past me is an option." I am slowly shaking my head side to side.

"I swear to God, I will tackle your senior citizen ass if you make a run for it, and I can't promise we won't both end up in the basement if that happens. Indiana Jones, I am not."

The tension of the situation dissipates quickly. I believe she understands exactly what I have just said. She lays her head back down and at least feigns acceptance.

"So, I'll tell you how my hostage situation ended, and then we can see how your hostage situation ends, ok girl?"

"I couldn't say how much time had passed from when I realized that I hadn't been shot to when I heard the lead hoodlum shout, 'ten minutes people, don't make a move for ten minutes, and this will all be over.'

"I just sit there with the girls. 'So brave...you girls are so, so brave. Such good girls,' I'm talking out loud now and repeating the same mantra over and over again. I don't make a move to get up. I'm not even sure that I can get up. My legs have fallen asleep and feel thick and dense below my waist. Then I hear a voice speaking close by in a concerned but soothing tone.

"'Are you and the kids ok, ma'am? Can I help you get up?' I look up and see a man approximately my age squatting down at the edge of the jewelry counter.

"'We're gonna help you up, ma'am.' I hear a voice coming from over my shoulder. I turn my head, and there is a police officer bending down to assist the old woman who had been laying on the floor to my right. She is openly weeping now, and I notice that her arm is covered in blood.

"'We need an EMT here,'" I hear the officer say.

"'Ok, ma'am,' the officer is back behind the counter and standing next to me. 'Let's get you guys up off the floor. Are any of you hurt?' he asks me as he reaches a hand under my elbow and forearm and places his other hand behind my daughter's back. For the first time I notice that I have a splitting headache and feel like I am going to throw up.

"'No,' I tell him, 'we're fine,' which is both the truth and a far cry from the truth.

"Later that day, as I exit the police station, my father pats me on the back and says, 'Well, you're in one piece, and that's behind you now.' His words, no doubt, are meant to bolster and console me. What I hear behind the words is what I've heard my whole life: vulnerability is weakness, weakness causes suffering, and this family doesn't suffer; we persevere. But my father is right about one thing, for the moment I am in one piece. What he doesn't see is that like a windshield with a stone chip, I am fracturing. For the time being, though, I will mortar myself together with an old family recipe handed down through the generations, one to the next, consisting of control, denial, overachievement and alcohol. I will add my own personal touches of nicotine and food addiction. There will, however, be no pity party for one, let alone taking the time to process what just happened here. If I don't acknowledge it, it isn't happening, right?" I look up at the dog in the mow and smile.

Don't Close Your Eyes,
It's a Fast Ride

Of all the dogs that have been in our family, Louie has made the biggest impact on our lifestyle. Nothing and I mean absolutely nothing that isn't nailed down or made of steel is safe in his proximity. Even with vigorous warnings to humans and regular reprimands for Louie, he is absolutely delighted by anyone's negligence. His precocious nature has been both a source of amusement and bone of contention between my husband and I. It is impossible to stay mad at Louie for long because of his sweet, docile personality. His most recent victim has apparently been the college student who rides at our farm and has just spent the weekend taking care of the dogs while we took the train to Chicago for the weekend. The minute we walk in, I can tell she's upset. "So, did the dogs torture you?" I ask her, and she can't wait to unburden herself.

"So, yesterday, I ran to go get food, and when I pulled back in the driveway, I see Louie and Kaya in a rigorous game of tug-o-war with my newly purchased Victoria's Secret bra. That was upsetting enough," she says tearfully, "but when I picked all my stuff up out of the yard and took it inside to put it away, one of the boys had lifted their leg and peed all over my suitcase. I'm certain I shut the door," she quickly adds, "but I left my suitcase open on the floor," she sighs, visibly upset again. I offer her an extra $40.00 for her troubles. She utters the token words of resistance, saying it's her own fault (and I agree), but eventually says, "Ok," which I knew she would.

The strength and function of Louie's back leg could now, a year or so after our meeting, be described as normal. His frame that started out carrying a mere sixty-nine pounds, now weighs-in just shy of one-hundred. His all-time favorite activity when we are home is a belly-rubbing session, and when we're not home, its counter-surfing. He has eaten numerous loaves of bread, thawing meat, bags of chips and a box of replacement ink cartridges for the printer. He has chewed up furniture, destroyed numerous dog toys, de-stuffed beds and left an entire laundry basket of my underwear crotch-less.

One afternoon, after returning home from our local Sam's Club, I put all of my purchases away and walk out to the barn with a new bag of cat food to re-fill the feeders. I am away from the house for maybe fifteen minutes. "What the hell?" I yell, breaking into a jog as I head back toward the house. Instead of going inside, I walk the length of the deck, and let myself into the fenced-in yard. As I round the corner of the house, I see Louie, lying contentedly in his favorite spot, grinning at me with the remains of a demolished cardboard box scattered at his front feet. Swirling around the yard in the wind, creating a bizarre sensory experience, are all two hundred 'Mountain Fresh' dryer sheets, set free from the folded confines of the box. Sometimes I get pissed-off, and sometimes I laugh. Today I laugh.

"I'd like to start a non-profit," I tell Denny resolutely over breakfast and wait for his reaction.

"I don't know if you haven't been paying attention or are in complete denial," he says slowly and carefully, looking directly at me, "But you've been running a non-profit for over twenty years, Laura." He smirks.

"Very funny," I shake my head. "I mean a real, legitimate non-profit. This economy is killing people; actually, it's killing animals. Look at a dog like Louie. Someone started out with great intentions; he was neutered and had his dewclaws out. He's a purebred. Someone paid good money for him," I continue, "so what went wrong? I keep asking myself, did someone lose their job? Did they see him and know they couldn't afford to help him? People are surrendering their family pets in record numbers, Denny. They're losing their homes, the whole family, including the pets. People are struggling. They're trying to figure out how to feed their kids, not get foreclosed on, and pay their living expenses. Should a family under duress have to lose their pet too? Should little Jimmy or Susie, who are already listening to mommy and daddy fight about money, not be able to pet their dog because dogfood no longer fits into the budget? There has to be a way to help," I say sighing, "there has to be something that good people with money can do to help good people in hard times."

"Don't you think you have enough on your plate?" he asks.

"Hmmmm," is my answer.

The Reveal

I walk through the local veterinarian's office with certain privileges, like not having to always stop at the front desk and make a request. Today I am here for horse medication, so I exchange pleasantries with the front desk staff and continue to the back of the clinic where one of the technicians will get what I need out of the closet. My familiarity here is the result of a number of factors; the first, being the sheer number of years I have been a client and the number of animals that are in my care and subsequently in their care. Other factors include a close, working relationship and friendship with the veterinarians and a few of the staff, including one of my best friends who is the Practice Manager.

As I stroll through, I poke my head into my girlfriend's office to say "hello." Our habit is to make a pledge to find the time to get together, but we rarely do. My life is stuffed full with the obligations of running a twenty-two stall horse facility, coaching the inter-collegiate riding team for Michigan State University, babysitting, volunteering at the hospital with Rose, an endless array of dog responsibilities, and now the leg work involved in getting a non-profit off the ground. She is juggling a full-time, forty-hour a week job, a husband and young son, and commissions for both her animal portrait work and her model horse painting. It always tickles me to be friends with this humble woman who is such an amazingly talented artist. "Let's find some time to grab dinner one night," I say, turning to head out.

"Sounds good, I could use a break," she laments.

Just as I am rounding the corner to leave the bustle of the back of the clinic where all the real medical work takes place, someone calls out my name.

"Hey, Laura, can I talk to you a minute?" asks one of the older technicians. She is close to my age.

"Sure, what's up?" I ask. I know I won't have to say much; this one's a talker.

"My sister-in-law called me just last night. I don't know if you know, but my brother died several years ago, and then after him, their dog died, so my sister-in law's been alone a really long time. Well, anyway, I've been trying to talk her into getting another dog for years now. She's retired and other than a daughter and two grandkids that she sees a few days a week, she sits in her house alone. She's been telling me for years she's not ready, so you coulda knocked me over with a feather when she called last night to say that she thinks it's time for her to have a dog in her life again. I asked her, "why now?" and she said because she keeps having a dream about a Labrador.......a yellow Labrador....so if you know of.........," her voice trails off, and her eyes and mouth pop wide open. "He isn't, is he?" she asks, wearing her incredulous expression.

"No, he isn't!" I answer back just as incredulously.

"Oh, no, I didn't think so," she says, pulling her chin back and shaking her head almost as if she were scolding herself for implying that I would give my beloved dog away. "But if you hear of a lab--" She is talking fast now and backing away, "let me know."

"Will do," I wave half-heartedly and walk out of the clinic.

I've got my horse medication, my truck is running, but I can't seem to make myself leave the clinic. I am staring out the windshield.

"Is something wrong?" Denny looks up from his phone.

"I don't think so," I answer, "I'm just trying figure out how something feels." Denny doesn't respond.

"I'll be back," I say and hop back out of the truck and head back into the clinic. I once again breeze past the front office staff and into the back. The woman I had just been talking to freezes and stares at me. I stretch my arm toward her and hand her a business card with my mobile phone number on it. "I think your sister-in-law and I are supposed to talk. Can you ask her to give me a call if she'd like to talk about Lou?" I am choking on the end of my sentence.

"Sure," is all she says with the same shocked look on her face.

I pull out of the clinic, and we drive home in silence.

My heart starts clanging the moment my phone rings, and I know it's the woman calling about Louie. Of course, she sounds articulate and polite as she asks if she is speaking with Laura. If she sounded any other way, I would shut this conversation down in thirty seconds. But I don't, and we talk for almost an hour. She tells me, with poised emotion, about the loss of her husband, and then their beloved dog five years later. She quietly and thoughtfully reflects about the pain of those losses, and without her ever saying, it is understood the only man in her life is gone, and there will never be another. She talks openly about her unwillingness to enter too quickly back into a relationship with a dog, and

I can sense that her canine companion is much more than a pet. She tells me that she was recently matched up with a dog through her local humane society, but that had not been successful, and she did not want to endure another failure. Maybe she shouldn't get another dog, she thought, until she had the dream. I chuckle and tell her I'm not sure if Louie is the Labrador that dreams are made of. I tell her all of his rotten Labrador behaviors, I tell her all of his endearing qualities, and I tell her his story of near death and how hard he fought to stay alive.

"Oh, my gosh, that's an amazing story, Laura. He sounds like an amazing dog. You can't give him to me after all you two have been through," she says. "he's obviously meant to be with you. God bless you for saving him."

For a moment I don't say anything. "Laura?" she asks, are you still there?"

"Yes, I am," I answer back but pause again. These goddamn tears seem to plague me. I wipe my eyes but try to keep them out of my voice.

"I'm sure that after everything you've been through, three-and-a-half years together…… and all of the money that you've spent on him……," she trails off trying to help me end the conversation.

"Carol," I begin, "talking to you has made it crystal clear to me why Louie came into my life. He and I were absolutely meant to be together. I also suffered a huge loss when my mother died very unexpectedly eleven months before meeting him. Louie gave me something to focus on, and helping him heal helped me heal too; it was kinda like group therapy at my house. But, I can honestly say, now that you and I have talked, I understand that Louie's been your

189

dog all along. The Universe just passed him through me on his way to you. He's part of the pack here, and I love him, love what he's done for me, for all of us, but it's obvious to me........." I try to swallow the large lump that's formed in my throat, "he's not meant to stay with us. I will honor his calling, and his calling is to be your special boy. It would be purely selfish for me to deny either one of you that."

"I don't know what to say," the emotion is thick in her voice.

"Say, yes, you'd finally like to meet your yellow dog," I answer, tears streaming down my face as I stroke Louie's rabbit fur head. He is dozing contentedly next to me on the kitchen floor.

We spend another half an hour discussing the particulars of his impending transition: what he eats and when, how often he goes outside to go potty, what he likes to play with, his favorite treats, where he sleeps, how long he sleeps and what size crate he will be comfortable in. She tells me her yard is not fenced, and I am instantly concerned, "he's already been a lost and broken dog once," I say, "and I have no doubt he'd be a runner if the opportunity presented itself........" I trail off. I can feel it behind my words but can't say for sure what it is: a patronizing ego, perhaps, that thinks I am the only one who can *really* take care of this dog? The thought of him leaving has me, the small me, suddenly feeling insecure and judgmental, and it is threatening to spoil this opportunity.

"I was planning on having a cable off my deck," she explains in a calm, kind tone, "and I wouldn't leave him alone, but I understand with all he's been through, if you aren't comfortable with the idea of me not having a fenced-in yard."

She is the milk of human kindness and you are being a bitch, I think to myself.

"No, no, I don't mean to sound like that. I know you won't let anything happen to him," I pause for a moment to gather my thoughts. "This is a new experience for me. I've always thought of the dogs as mine......forever. I know Louie is meant to be with you, and if for some reason it doesn't work out, or it's not what you thought it would be, he will always have a home here. I just had a moment of panic." I laugh nervously, "three-and- a-half years is a long time to be a foster mom."

We make plans to bring Louie to her home on the upcoming Sunday. I tell her I will bring Louie's food dish and enough food to last him at least a full week. "Would you like your family to meet him?" I ask.

"Not yet. I want Louie and I to have a chance to get acquainted, and I don't want my grandsons to be disappointed if for some reason it didn't work out. I'd like to give it a day or so before they meet him." I understand completely.

Put up, or Shut Up

It is 5:00 am, and I am staring at the blank computer screen with tears rolling down my face. "I realize, mom, you are probably in some sort of transition……" my words come out as a strangled whisper, "but the rest of you sitting up there watching this need to give me a little help here…..I'm begging you." I am sending out this plea mainly to my long-deceased grandparents, but will accept assistance from anyone on that side of the life veil with inspiring words or a good idea. I close my eyes, put my face in my hands and take a deep breath to settle myself. I focus on the air going in and out of my body. I will myself to get out of my own head and channel the wisdom and inspiration I know the Universe holds. Even the dogs are reverently quiet, scattered around me on the floor of the living room, with the exception of Rose, who has been standing next to me, my steadfast companion, resting her head on my lap while I absently work my fingers through her thick, white fur.

The spirits do not disappoint me! The writing of my mother's eulogy flows out of me freely once I start. I am smiling as I type what most people at this gathering already know, that my mother knew no strangers and will no doubt arrive in Heaven chatting. When I hit the "print" command on the computer screen, I am satisfied with what I will share later in the morning.

The church is packed full of people. My mother's body has been brought from the funeral home and is staged in the large vestibule at the front of the church. A few times this morning I have had brief moments when I felt unsteady on my feet. I envision these episodes as my body enduring a series of internal quakes, caused no doubt by the fracturing of my heart. The family stands around in solemn conversation while more than two hundred mourners are seated in the sanctuary of this beautiful old church. I feel no connection to organized religion but can appreciate those, like my mother, who have come here with the best of intentions and find some measure of comfort inside these walls.

We are waiting to be taken back to the family waiting area so that Reverend Silver Tongue can deliver his final directives regarding the funeral program. My husband's ex-wife is standing with their two daughters and talking with my sister. Originally, at my urging, and wholeheartedly supported by my parents, my husband's ex-wife has for the past several years has been included in all of the holiday gatherings that have taken place at their home. She has been a participant in the discussions of who is bringing what passing dishes for meals, included in our family gift exchange, and, like the rest of my parent's flock, on Christmas day has received an envelope with a hundred dollars cash enclosed.

My mother shared my belief that we all need to belong to a pack. The quality of our existence and survival depend on it. Because my husband and his ex-wife have children together, and now a grandchild whose lives we all share, she is part of our pack. Before we are sequestered away, I request that she stay with her girls and our grandson who is confused and devastated by my mother's disappearing act, and be seated with them in the family rows at the front of the church.

The Reverend never misses a beat. Everyone in attendance is captivated by the story of my mother's life. After a brief introduction explaining my mother's parentage, he moves on to the exciting and romantic details of my parent's first meeting on a blind date to watch a basketball game. They are in Bremerhaven, Germany. My father is stationed at the United States Air Force base, and my mother is visiting her mother and step-father, who is an art teacher in an American school.

The Reverend is describing for us what sounds like a scene out of a romantic comedy as he retells a story my father shared with him during his home visit. The year is 1956, and my mother, a young woman of twenty and now engaged to my father, is travelling from Germany to Italy to visit a family friend during the unforeseen start of The Hungarian Uprising. He tells how my father desperately seeks the permission of his superior officers to bring her back to Germany and the safety of the U.S. base.

I am reminded of how my father appeared to me as child: handsome, commanding, and larger-than-life, as the story goes on to describe him finding my mother and protecting her while they navigated their way back to safety through military check-points and railroad cars packed to their limits with panicked and distraught refugees. *Our lives pass in the blink of an eye,* I am thinking, as I pat the boney thigh of the frail old man who is sitting next to me nodding his head and weeping at the memory of that distant time, now himself an anguished widower.

My hands begin to tremble as the Reverend wraps up my mother's family history. "Not about me…. not about me…. not about me," is my current mantra. In a moment, he will nod my way, and I will have to, "get my shit together" like never before. I have already decided that I will exit the pew facing forward so that I do not see the somber faces watching me as I make my way into uncharted territory. I have calculated what I believe to be an accurate estimate of the number of steps it will take for me to get from the end of the pew to the pulpit, the habit of a horse trainer who has spent decades walking the distances between jumps. "Walk slowly, breathe slowly, speak slowly," I am telling myself, "ignore the sweaty palms, damp underarms and clanging heart." This is my eulogy strategy.

As I take the final step that places me in front of the microphone, I set my single sheet of white paper on the podium and just stare at it. I take a step backwards and hear the Reverend somewhere from behind me quietly say, "take your time."

I am shivering deep down inside, but my armpits are damp with sweat. I am staring at the floor. I force a deep breath but do not move. "This is interesting," I think to myself, as a comforting warm wash surrounds me. I wonder briefly if I am passing out. I am alone. Everything around me has faded into the background. I hear a voice close to my ear. "These are important words, Laura. For one person, whose heart will hear them today, they hold the power of change. You asked for our help, now we are asking for yours.

Share the words." It is a directive from my grandmother, spoken in her voice with her matter-of-fact style.

Still looking down, I nod my head and whisper, "Of course you're here," and her strong, familiar presence bolsters me in this moment. I can, literally, feel her arm around me and the pressure of her gentle shove that has me taking a definitive step towards the podium. I lift my eyes and, for a long moment, just gaze out at the crowd. Before I speak the first word, I silently invite my mother to share the view. Together we are looking at a sea of people she loved.

I have titled the eulogy, "Certainties about My Mother" and numbered each point, one through nine. As I am speaking, some points are met with head nodding acknowledgement, like when I make the statement that my mother knew no strangers. Others points arouse soft laughter through the crowd when I mention that my sister and I have just inherited the largest, privately owned collection of holiday sweaters in North America, and Alfred Dunner Sportswear and Clark Shoes will soon be experiencing significant slumps in their mid-west sales. I try to engage my best public speaking skills and make eye contact in several different areas of the vast sanctuary, but it is ultimately my daughter's face my eyes settle on when I speak about my mother's deep appreciation for the intrinsic flow of life and how she would be the first person to appreciate that her time to leave this earth is also another's time to arrive. I conclude; "My mother often remarked that she lived a wonderful life. So, from my mother's heart to your hearts, please, go live your wonderful life. She loved you all."

Welcome Home

I am driving slowly through the middleclass subdivision cussing, "Why in the fuck don't people put big, clearly-visible house numbers up anymore? They don't want the police or fire department to be able find them if they call for help?" I am squinting at mailboxes.

"Where are *our* big, clearly visible house numbers?" Denny asks deadpan from the passenger seat.

"Shut up," is the best I got.

Louie is in the back seat looking intently out the window like he's trying to help me. "You're a good dog, Lou," I tell him looking in the rearview mirror, "more help than some people I know," and I shoot Denny a narrow-eyed scowl.

"This is it," Denny says gesturing to the house we are approaching on the right. I confirm the numbers, which actually are clearly visible, and pull into the driveway.

"Are you coming in with us?" I ask Denny.

"Nope," he says, "I'll be right here when you're done. Here's the adoption agreement," and he hands me the white envelope.

"Come on, Lou," I whisper as I snap the leash onto his collar. He is sitting in the back seat, facing me with rapt attention like a school student anxiously awaiting his chance to be called-on to take a turn at a favorite game. *Pick me, pick me, pick me,* he seems to be saying. "You've already been picked, buddy," I say somberly. "You're not on my team anymore." I stroke his ears and smooch the end of his nose.

"Aren't you the one who always says, 'they know exactly what we're saying?' Denny says, glancing over his shoulder.

I hate when he parrots my words back to me.

Louie and I make our way to the front walkway, and I rap my knuckles on the edge of the storm door. A few seconds later it opens, and there stands Carol looking exactly like she sounded on the phone. She greets both of us warmly and invites us in. Louie is more intent on inspecting his physical surroundings than he is in meeting the resident human, "typical dog behavior," I say, feeling a little bad that he isn't more interested in meeting her, "we're chopped liver until they need something," I shrug. "Can I let him go?" I ask, "He's very interested in checking the house out."

"Oh, of course," she says.

Louie lays his nose on the ground and moves about the house. His awkward gait is something between an amble and a gallop as he checks out every surface high and low that's within his nose's reach. Carol and I walk through the house and into the living room where she asks me to look at the size of her crate and shows me the area available to Louie in her currently snow-covered backyard. She has shoveled off the deck and a small area for him to go potty. "I plan to walk in the neighborhood for exercise," she explains, and I remind her he will need some work on how to be polite at the end of a leash. Louie joins us in the living-room and stares out the sliding glass door, taking in all of the new scenery for a minute or two before turning around and resuming his perusal of the inside of the house. Carol and I chat easily for the next ten or fifteen minutes. She shares with me that she is a retired nurse. She lives a simple life, likes to stay close to home and her favorite activity, clearly obvious by the look of extreme pleasure on her face, is spending time with her grandchildren. This is a task that she and Louie will do together.

"He loves to ride in the car," I remind her.

"I see you brought me some paperwork," she nods at the envelope, slightly creased from my, until now, unperceived death grip.

"Oh, yep," I look down at my hand as though I'm not quite sure how an envelope materialized there. *Holy shit, I'm giving my dog away to someone I don't even know.* "This is the adoption agreement. I'll have you sign it while I'm here…….. but……..I'm so sorry," I look up at her apologetically, tears brimming in my eyes, "paragraph six is the return policy, he always has a home," I stop talking and hand her the papers. Louie is sitting next to me, leaning into my leg. I am stroking his head, talking myself out of grabbing the leash and making a run for it.

"I appreciate how diligent you are about making sure he'll always be taken care of." Her smile is warm and sincere.

"Thank you," I croak.

It's quiet in the house for a minute while she reads over the adoption contract and fills in the spaces that prompt her for initials or signatures. She has already prepared a check and hands it to me now with the completed paperwork. I glance at it and see that it is made out for more than the agreed upon adoption fee and don't trust myself to speak but give her an appreciative smile. Reflecting back on all the occurrences that have led up to this moment has me feeling like an emotional kaleidoscope. I am holding in my hand a check made out to Love from Louie, a registered 501c3 non-profit that I founded, and I am handing Louie off to the woman who will be his future. I am feeling overwhelmed. I squat down, squeeze Louie's rabbit fur ears and kiss him on top of the head. "Please call if you have any questions or problems," I say in a squeaky voice, "and let me know how he's doing." We all walk to the door, and Carol reaches over and hugs me.

"He's an answer to my prayer," she whispers, and I smile into her shoulder.

As I step back and prepare to leave, I reach down and grab the leash that is still attached to Louie's collar and hand it to Carol. "He probably thinks he's supposed to leave with me," I say quietly, "until he figures out he belongs to you now." I squat in front of Louie and stare into his face, willing him to read my mind. *This is an important assignment, buddy. You have to take care of her, Ok? And be a good boy, Lou. I love you. Big Lou, you da man!* I close my eyes and kiss him on his cold, wet nose. When I open my eyes, Louie's eyes are still locked with mine, and there it is, illuminated in the Milk Dud brown windows to his soul, the perfection of the Universe.

We are a few blocks away from Carol's house, and I cannot stop crying. "Will you see if there's a napkin in the glove box?" I ask Denny when I stop the car at a red light. After handing me the napkin, which is already a soggy wad full of snot and tears, I happen to glance over at the car pulled up next to us: the woman driving is glaring over at Denny. "Look at the car next to us," I say to Denny, who immediately glances over.

"Oh, terrific, she thinks *I'm* an asshole," he says melodramatically and looks over at me, eyebrows raised.

"Amazing, she can read you so accurately at a glance," I reply sarcastically, laughing now.

Carol begins texting me pictures of Louie right away. I am not surprised as the days go by that her grandsons are now present in them, hugging, playing and sitting on the floor with Louie watching television. She reports that everyone is completely enamored with everyone else. Several times I go back and look at one of the pictures where Louie is sporting his full-faced, goofy grin, and I am touched and relieved. Louie is safe and at home in the love of his family. Louie's departure from my life, although he is still very much alive, has me reflecting on something I once said to my mother and have repeated many times since then: you can't change an exit. The day I said that to her, I was referring to death, but as I reflect on my half-century in this lifetime, I understand that our brief stay here is actually a series of beginnings and endings, each transition offering us either respite or prompting us to expand our human experience. Louie's time with me wasn't a moment longer than it was meant to be. Our relationship allowed me to (somewhat) gracefully expand in a way I never really have before; Louie's departure from my everyday life wasn't through death, it was a decision; one that was outside the realm of any previous experience I'd had with a dog.

I have always viewed my family pets as lifelong relationships. My montage of experiences with Louie have gifted me a leap of awareness, one that challenges me to elaborate on my personal and spiritual definition of 'guardian' and to clarify my intentions going forward as a non-profit.

I will forever be grateful to the buttercup yellow dog for arriving into my life so humbly with his lessons in healing and purpose. I vow not to forget what Louie and the pack have demonstrated so beautifully: that finding purpose and lasting transformation isn't a struggle born in ambitious, animated, self-indulgence, but rather, true purpose reveals itself in the deep peace of acceptance, the faith of letting go and the simplicity of gratitude. Regardless of what compels us to surrender and however brief those tranquil moments might be, magic always happens there.

All In

I pull the ringing phone out of my pocket. "I'm really close now, Mom," I say almost in a whisper. "Give me another thirty. I hope you'll hear from me first."

Sitting on this mow with my legs crossed, balancing my weight against the incline, has made my butt, legs and back stiff. Slowly, I lower my upper body down until I am resting on my side, head and neck in the palm of my right hand. I slide my phone back into my pocket. I stretch my legs out too, until they are almost straight. There is a momentary flash of uneasiness when I briefly play the devil's advocate with myself. Have I been here so long that I'm getting careless?

"Oh, the irony," I say, looking up at the dog in her nest, using my dramatic news-anchor voice, "woman spends hours climbing to abandoned dog, talking non-stop. Dog gets even by ripping woman's throat out."

I give her a wry smile, "I think that's called gallows humor." Her eyes bounce up and make brief contact with mine.

"Ok, admittedly not funny," I apologize to her.

"I'm 'all in' girl. I roll on to my belly and prop my weight on my elbows and make the quotation gesture with my fingers.

"I'm not walking away alone today. No matter how long we have to spend on this damp, stinky mow, we're leaving together. Even if you growl at me or show me your teeth, I'm gonna wait you out. I've learned a lot of things since that day in the jewelry store: My life is a direct reflection of what I'm sending out to the world. You know the old adage: you can't get what you can't give. Well, I have been the recipient of abundant love, abundant patience and abundant acceptance. I have spent the past thirty days sharing those gifts with you, and here we are, the elusive dweller of the woods and the interloper, less than ten feet apart.

"This would be an excellent time to run down and greet me," I tell her. "Admittedly yes, I would love for this to end like a Purina dog food commercial. Speaking of food, I see you like the food you've been eating. It's been a fair trade, don't you think? Me feeding your physical body and you feeding my emotional body."

As I am talking to her, I am on my belly ungracefully pulling myself towards her nest on my elbows.

"For every shitty thing that's ever happened to you, I'm sorry. This is a fresh start." I continue my ascent up the straw. I am within five or so feet of her now. I am momentarily out of words, so I just keep creeping toward her until I am within an arm's stretch from her hindquarters. Her head is glued to the edge of her nest, and she is watching me intently but not holding my gaze. Her eyes are busy going back-and-forth between looking at me and not looking at me.

I can reach her now. We are less than two feet apart. I pull my right hand down, and with my left hand I slowly remove my leather glove. She is watching me.

"I want to feel your warmth, momma, and I want you to feel mine."

I rest my arm on the straw, and as I slowly reach toward her, I turn my head slightly so that I am showing her some deference.

"I'm gonna touch you now, girl," I tell her as I start to reach toward her body. "Tell her, Angels and Spirits, tell her Fairies. Tell her everything is going to be just fine now."

Most dogs hate having their feet touched, so I let my hand skim over her leg and softly settle on her hip. I doubt that either of us is breathing in this moment.

"I love you," Is all I can think to say to her as I slowly begin to caress her hip, "I love you," and I cannot help myself, I begin to cry. I lay the side of my head down on my arm and let the tears and sobs come out of me as I caress her hip and back. Her response to my emotional display is better than any movie script ever written. My angel in the woods lifts her weight up just enough to reposition her body so she is facing me and begins licking my hand.

"Oh my God," I am bawling now. "Hi, beautiful," I coo to her as I scratch behind her ear. The relief is palpable. She is echoing my joy and relief by whimpering and licking her approval.

We revel in the physical presence of each other. I am rubbing my hands all over her face and body. After a few minutes of this celebration tick by, I pull off my other glove, reach in my jacket pocket and pull out my cell phone. It is hard to focus because of the tears and ruined make-up. I hit redial and listen to the ring.

"Hellooo," says my mother. Already giddy, I burst out laughing at my mother's Mrs. Doubtfire sounding greeting.

"We're together, Mom. Can you believe it? We're finally together!"

"Oh, honey, I'm so relieved, for both of you. What should we do now?" she asks.

"Will you meet me at the farm? We can take her into the clinic so they can check her out," I ask, already knowing what her answer will be.

"You bet. I'm on my way," she says. "I'm so excited to meet her," she adds before hanging up.

"Alright girl, let's blow this popsicle stand," I say to the dog. I continue to lie on the ground with her while I reach into my right jacket pocket and pull out the slip leash. I am relieved that this time it does not seem to cause her any stress. I carefully slip it over her ample jowls and head and pull myself up to a sitting position.

"We're outta here" I tell her, and she willingly follows me as I scoot down the length of the straw mow on my butt. Arriving together at the bottom, it takes me a moment of standing before I feel like I have my land legs back. I offer her the dry food in the bowl again, but she's not interested in eating at the moment. I notice that she has obviously been a mommy before, several times by the look of her sagging teats, but now is not the time to bring that up.

"Ok, girl, we aren't too far from lunch now" I assure her.

I gather up the bowl and water bottle and put them back into the plastic bag.

"Any parting words?" I ask her. "No?" Well, then, let's get going. Grandma Pat is waiting to meet you."

We head toward the door, but as we cross the threshold, she panics, spins and heads back into the barn.

"No girl, not back in here," I tell her, and apply a little pressure on the leash. Her response is to sit down and do her best to reverse herself out of the make-shift collar.

"Hey, easy girl," I coo to her and bend over and rub her head and shoulders until I see her body relax a bit.

And then it dawns on me; "You don't like to be seen in the daylight, do you girl? I ask her. "That's how you've managed to survive here undisturbed for so long." For a few moments we stand, silent and stationary, looking out from the opening of the barn. My fingertips are stroking the length of her body.

"I understand exactly where you're coming from, girl. It's a gigantic leap of faith to expose yourself......." My words trail off as I continue to stare out at nothing in particular in the rain- soaked woods.

"So, have I told you I believe this is hell?" I pause, as if waiting her reply.

"That this earthy plane is the 'down below' to the 'up above' we call Heaven. I think our purpose here is to hold the light of our presence, however flickering, and illuminate the darkness that is prevalent here. Our journey is about the light. To protect our light, to love our light, to accept our flame for its individual perfection. When our light is strong, it can't help but shine into the space of others. That's what you and I are doing right now, sharing our lights.

"Oscar Wilde said it best, 'We are all in the gutter, but some of us are looking at the stars.' "So, there you have it. I think I've got at least part of this figured out, and maybe it will help you; I don't deny my past, but I've had to learn to let it go to not let it define my future. Like you walking away from this barn, I had to learn that every day I am living, I walk out into the world, and I can be exactly what I decide to be, as grateful or as sorrowful as I choose. It really is as simple as that."

I reposition myself so I am in a sumo-wrestler-like stance. "Trust" is the only word I say as I reach my arms around her butt and chest and lift her off the ground.

"You couldn't let me do this when you were a skinny girl, huh?" I am laughing as I tip my head toward my shoulder, trying to see the path that leads to the road around her ample head and body. After a few staggering steps I find my balance point and begin moving forward. I am singing to her as we make the trek together through the woods, "This little light of yours, we're gonna see it shine, this little light of yours, we're gonna see it shine, hmmm, hmmm, hmmm hmm hmm….hmmm, hmmm, hmm……….."

Don't Let Go

After the funeral, my siblings and I host a small group of family and our mother's closest friends at our father's condominium. It is almost unbearable for me to break the plane of this front doorway and not have my mother pop out of the kitchen to greet me. The gathering is flat and sad, and I am grateful it doesn't last very long. My father has already fixed himself a Manhattan and very soon the bourbon-laden sadness will be more than I can stand. My brother and one of his daughters are going to stay with him for the first few nights. I am relieved to have the excuse of animals at home so that I can make my exit.

I walk up the steps to the door of our home with lead feet. I pause, waiting for my husband to catch up and walk through the gate so I can latch it behind him. We have a system for entering and exiting our home that has become second nature, designed to keep our four-legged companions from, in my husband's words, "breaking wide." I let him walk through the door first and into the house where the dogs are assembled for their usual enthusiastic greeting. My husband grumbles his usual, "get back! get back!" while making a "shooing" gesture with his hands. His back to me, I sigh, roll my eyes and proceed to have my customary wrestling match to close the weather-beaten storm door.

"I'm gonna go upstairs and change. Do you need anything?" my husband asks. I answer with something between a hum and a mumble as he heads towards the stairs. The dogs are still gathered around me, each one with its own distinct personality and motive. One is sitting quietly in front of me staring at my face with her soft brown eyes, waiting to be acknowledged. One is bumping me with her dry, rough nose, demanding attention, and the others are sniffing the uncommon scents of people, food and places embedded in the fabric of my clothing. One of my daughter's friends once made the comment during a visit home from college, "Wow, your mom has replaced you with dogs," and we all laughed.

Animals have surrounded me for my entire life, but during the past year or so, I began to appreciate them on a completely new and more intimate level. I had always seen the dogs in my adult life as a daily responsibility, rewarded by their antics, loyalty and companionship. My somewhat one-dimensional view as a caregiver was undergoing a transformation, bringing back into my life some of the simplicity and genuineness I had experienced during my interactions with them as a child, when they were literally my closest friends, confidantes and almost constant companions.

With total disregard for my new black outfit, I sit down on the kitchen floor and lean against the cupboards. Housekeeping has been neglected for several days now. The kitchen floor is filthy, covered with grime tracked in by several sets of paws and is accompanied by copious amounts of dog hair wafting across the tile. Emerging on the tile floor has caused a flurry of renewed activity as the dog's clamor around, each one wanting to be as close to me as possible. Sitting on the floor in my now rumpled, dirty and dog-hair-covered funeral attire, I burst into tears. "I really need some help, guys" I say to the dogs, sobbing. I am hugging necks and bodies, and squishing and kissing the faces of those that are closest to me. "I have absolutely no idea where I go from here. I don't feel like me anymore…." Once again I am overwhelmed by a deep sense of loss and grief. "You're all experts at survival," I say incredulously as the words flow out of my mouth. I reach out and deliberately touch each dog, whispering their names like a prayer, "Kaya, Rose, Otis, Buddy, Chi-Chi, Angel Momma………" I trail off, overwhelmed by both loss and love. "Oh my god, I'm living in a house with survival experts!" I am choking on my words, blubbering now at this astounding revelation. I have already been a front row observer to this troupe's capacity to endure life's rough spots, have watched their miraculous ability to heal and to move on gracefully with their lives. "Yes," I cry enthusiastically to the group, holding my arms wide open as they writhe and wiggle, tails wagging and tongues licking, "please rescue me!" And they do.

Epilogue

*I came out alone on my way to my tryst. But who
is this that follows me in the silent dark? I move
aside to avoid his presence but I escape him not.*

*He makes the dust rise from the earth with his swagger;
he adds his loud voice to every word that I utter.*

*He is my own little self, my lord, he knows no shame;
but I am ashamed to come to thy door in his company.*

~ Rabindranath Tagore

So, You Think This Is About You?

We're practically stealth, this dog and I. That is, of course, if you do not notice the faint squeak emanating from the curved rubber soles of my modern day "moon shoes" or the barely perceptible, occasional click of Roses' toenails making contact with the tile. I am, in this moment, exactly what I spend a significant amount of mental energy and money trying not to be: an average-looking, unattractively dressed, decidedly un-hip, stereotypical middle-aged woman. My oversized, Kelly green smock, that makes me look like I belong in an FTD florist commercial, along with the photo ID clipped to the lapel, identify me as a hospital volunteer, specifically, a Therapy Dog Handler. My companion, of course, is Rose. She is a breathtaking beauty, minimally clad in a red bandana, fluffy, white, double-layered fur coat and a set of soulful, dark eyes with golden highlights. Her photo ID is attached to a leather leash and identifies her as, you guessed it, the Therapy Dog.

We have traveled on the elevator to the sixth floor of the main hospital. This floor and the one above it are referred to by the staff as "Med-Surge" floors. The sixth and seventh floors are my favorite floors to visit because of the wide variety of patients. In these rooms lie the old, the young and the middle-aged; the dying, the recovering, the forgotten and the cherished.

Most people are startled or excited to see my large, regal companion emerging from an elevator or strolling down a hallway and feel immediately compelled to ask a question or make a comment. And so begins a visit with a therapy dog. One evening several weeks ago while on this floor, a young boy ran out into the hallway, and yelled to his mother, "Hey, there's a polar bear here on a leash!"

On this evening, though, the halls are practically empty with the exception of an occasional staff member walking by. No one is chatty. I wonder if the staff is bored or relieved to be working on a night such as this, without the usual hustle and noise level normally present on these floors. I have learned not to comment about the quiet. Nurses are a superstitious bunch.

I look down at my watch and make a mental decision that after we walk this hallway, Rose and I will head home. While I am still walking and looking down, I feel a tug of the leash. Stopping quickly, I realize that Rose is no longer walking beside me. She is standing still, staring across the hall into the open door of a patient room. I take the pace backwards to re-join her and look to see what has captured her attention. Sitting in the chair at the end of the hospital bed, staring out the window on the farthest side of the room is a petite, elderly-looking woman. "Hey girl, let's finish this hall," I say in a voice too loud for a hospital hallway, thinking maybe the woman will hear me and look our way. But she remains completely motionless in the chair, and Rose remains rooted in her spot. "Alright, beautiful, let's keep moving," I say again in my loud voice, patting Rose on the side, but once again the woman either doesn't hear me or doesn't want to hear me. For the minute or so that we have been standing here, the woman never shifts her body or moves her eyes away from whatever it is she sees through the glass of the window. I encourage Rose to "come," and after a gentle tug on the leash, she reluctantly follows me away from the open door.

We continue to the end of the dead-end hallway. Peering into the rooms with open doors, I can see the covered legs and feet of one or two patients lying in beds, but because no staff has suggested a room visit, and no visitors are present to make an initial contact, Rose and I turn around and backtrack toward the nurse's station and main hospital elevators. Rose and I do not enter a patient room unless someone had solicited the visit. Rose is much too big, and the rooms are far too crowded to walk in and find out that the patient is allergic to pet dander or deathly afraid of dogs.

No longer trolling for potential visiting encounters, I pick the pace up a bit, resolute in my decision to call it a night. We once again approach the mid-point of the hallway and the open door of the room where the woman is sitting in the chair. This time Rose does not stop but instead makes an unprecedented and very un-therapy dog like move: she walks across the front of my body and trots through the open door and directly into the room. Completely caught off guard, I frantically rap my knuckles on the wall and babble a greeting to announce our unorthodox entry into this space. Stunned, at this point, I simply follow my rogue therapy dog past the foot of two empty hospital beds and to the end of the room.

Walking quietly now but without hesitation, Rose maneuvers her large body between the narrow space at the end of the second bed and the side of the chair on which the woman is sitting. Once through the gap, she makes a ninety degree turn and positions herself directly in front of the woman. Rose is standing so close to the woman's body that the front of her chest is resting against the woman's knees. Rose is staring, soft-eyed and placid at the woman's face. The woman continues to sit perfectly still, and Rose mirrors her stillness. I am standing awkwardly off to the side of the chair, slightly behind the woman's right shoulder. I cannot see her face, only the back of her head with its stringy grey hair and her slightly stooped shoulders. Although she is clad in a heavy, tired-looking bathrobe, the body beneath it appears to be thin and frail. It is very uncharacteristic of me, especially in this setting, but I am stupefied and frozen with indecision. If a passerby were to look in on us, I imagine we would look like a hospital scene in a wax museum.

"Holy crap, Now what do I do?" I am wondering. I realize that dragging my ninety pound therapy dog out of a hospital room is probably counter- productive to our purpose. I decide to act as if nothing odd is taking place here and muster another attempt to introduce myself and my audacious companion. But my intended gesture is trumped by Rose, who gently lays her head down in the woman's lap. I freeze…..but nothing happens. The thought enters my mind that perhaps this patient is blind, deaf, or suffering from Alzheimer's or dementia. I cannot believe that Rose is so persistent about standing here with this woman. This has turned into a one dog show. Several minutes have elapsed now, and this woman has not even acknowledged that there is a giant white dog standing in front of her with the weight of her ample head resting in her lap. I am convinced the woman is sleeping. Dead people slump, don't they?

I am going to drag Rose out of here, I decide. Then, in an instant, the whole game changes as I watch disbelieving while the woman, very, very slowly, raises her right hand from the arm of the chair and lightly places it on the top of Rose's head. I notice how small the woman's hand looks, the size of a child's, but with boney, permanently crooked fingers. The skin on her hand and arm is dull and translucent, almost dirty looking with dark veins and age spots. I do not move and, momentarily, I do not breathe. Still not unlocking her gaze away from the windows, the woman gently begins to pat the top of Rose's head. Her touch is tentative at first, not because, I suspect, she is uncomfortable with Rose, but because she is coming into this moment from somewhere very far away from here.

Her left hand leaves the other arm of the chair and gently joins the right hand in lightly petting the top of Rose's head. I am still standing by the woman's right shoulder. I start to slowly kneel down by the side of the chair, and Rose's dark eyes narrow and look directly at mine. I stand back up and pray Rose will remain quietly engaged with the woman. Rose is still watching me, so I raise the palm of my hand toward her and silently mouth the word "stay." I return my arm to my side and take a deep breath as Rose's expression softens and turns away from me, her attention re-focusing on the woman in the chair. The patting of her head has turned into a caress, and the woman is using the full extension of her arms to slowly run her fingers through the thick, long hair on Rose's back and shoulders. "Fur therapy," I think to myself and smile.

I have sensed a shift and realize the woman is here now, at least present with Rose. She seems unaware that I am in the room. The woman leans forward now, bent over Rose's head that is still resting in her lap and encircles the front of Rose's with her frail body. I hear something. I am not sure what the sound is and for a moment I scan the room thinking it is a piece of medical equipment that I have not noticed or a staff member in the doorway. But there is no one here, no equipment in this room and nothing hooked up to this patient. As I look back at the scene in front of me, I realize that the noise is coming from the woman. She is crying, I think, and murmuring something. I cannot discern what she is saying, and I am aware that that these words are not meant for me. They are meant for either the vision in the window or for Rose. Either way, the words continue to flow out of the woman's mouth, a soft moaning, muffled by fur and emotion.

My throat is tight. I swallow hard and use my curled index fingers to pull down the lower lids of my eyes in an attempt to control the tears that threaten to spill over. I gaze upward and stare at nothing. The soft crying and murmuring has turned to sobbing now. The woman's frail body, clad in the old, faded blue terry cloth, heaves up and down against the top of Rose's head. I am stunned by how raw and desperate the sobbing sounds. I would not think a body this small and frail could hold a sorrow that sounds so immense. The woman's gnarled fingers are holding handfuls of Rose's thick, white fur. The clutching seems desperate, as if holding onto Rose is her only hope of staying anchored in this spot, not to be swept away in this sea of sadness. I fade back against the wall like a ghost witnessing this private, agonizing purging with tears streaming down my face.

Through the blur of my own emotion, I once again see Rose's eye staring at me from where her head is resting in the woman's lap, and once more I feel compelled to lift my hand and issue a silent command. My eyes are locked with Rose's eyes. Suddenly, as if emerging out of dense fog, my knees feel weak as I am astonished at the full impact of what is transpiring here. Rose's intense, unwavering gaze has silenced me. I realize now, that for the second time since entering this room tonight, Rose is compelling me to be still, to shut my mind off, to duct tape my ego and to realize my humanness has no place in this moment. My only purpose here tonight is to be a witness.

Gradually, the momentum of the woman's sobbing begins to ebb, and I hear her take a deep, ragged breath. She pulls herself up slightly, creating space between her body and Rose. The woman wipes her eyes and nose on the sleeve of her tired blue robe. She resumes the gentle stroking of Rose's head, and this time, when she speaks, her words are soft but clear, and I can hear her. "I seem to have gotten your head wet" she says, and uses the underside of the already used sleeve to wipe the dampness she feels on Rose's head. The woman takes notice of the hospital ID tag hanging motionless from the leather leash that is draped between my right hand and Rose's collar. Stroking Rose's chin now, I smile, deeply touched as I watch Rose raise her head with eyes closed, and accept all that is being offered here. "Rose", the woman says, cupping Rose's face in her hands and leaning forward so they are now nose to nose and eye to eye. "I have been here for thirteen days," she pauses, "and you are my first visitor. Thank you for coming to see me," she says, leaning in and gently kissing Rose on top of the head.

And with that our visit has ended. Rose stands up and looks at me, and I mumble, "good night" and walk out of the room, Rose obediently at my left side. We walk back into the deserted hallway and head for the elevators. I push the button, and I am staring at Rose when suddenly she cuts lose with a full body shake. I laugh out loud, amused and relieved as I recognize this gesture as "discharging," the spiritual practice of releasing energy that you have accumulated from someone you have had contact with, a dusting off of the soul, so to speak. The elevator doors slide open, and we step in. When the doors close, I bend down and pat Rose on her side, "Can I say something? You're my hero." She does not acknowledge my praise and continues standing quietly by my side. The elevator comes to a stop, and when the doors open, we exit into the main hospital lobby. I am relieved that it is empty. It is time to go home.